SAVVY INVESTING

STRATEGIES FOR SUCCESSFUL INVESTING

GARY D. LEMON

First published by Dog Ear Publishing
4011 Vincennes Rd
Indianapolis, IN 46268
www.dogearpublishing.net

ISBN: 978-1-4575-4822-2

This book is printed on acid-free paper.

Printed in the United States of America

To Susan, Mark, Michael, Beth, Meredith and Tessa

CONTENTS

ACKNOWLEDGEMENTS

Over the course of a lifetime many individuals have helped shape my understanding of investing. I have spent countless hours reading academic journals, going to professional meetings, reading books devoted to the topic of investing, talking to investment professionals, and helping students understand the world of investments. Each of these encounters has shaped my investment philosophy. Without each of these elements my understanding of how the market works would be greatly diminished.

Many of the individuals I have helped with their investing have encouraged me to write down what I had learned about investing. In addition, I had often thought I should write a book on investments to show my parents what I had learned and to help my sons become savvy investors. I never thought I had the time to write such a book until now.

When I started this project I knew it would not be easy; it has been even harder than I thought it would be. My wife, Susan has read every word more than once and has made innumerable suggestions that have improved the text. My friend, Cynthia Cornell, read the entire text at least three times, each time finding errors that I had let creep into the text; she also made many suggestions on how to make the text more readable. The editor at Dog Ear not only made corrections but also provided me with an outline for improving the book. I will be forever grateful for their help.

I would also like to thank Zachary Taylor, a DePauw University student, who created the artwork for the book. He took my ideas and was able to express them in cartoon form.

Thank you to all who have helped me become a savvy investor.

INTRODUCTION

WHY THIS BOOK?

Are you baffled by how the stock market works? Are you disappointed by the returns you have earned in the market? Do you want unbiased information about how the stock market *really* works? Do you want objective advice about how to invest your money? If so, *I am writing this book for you.*

In particular, I am writing this book for individuals who have little-to-moderate understanding of how the stock market works. You may be aware that you should be in the stock market but are afraid to take the leap because you are not sure where to start. Or you may currently be in the stock market but are disappointed in the returns you are earning and feel you are paying too much for the advice you are receiving. You may also want to have a deeper understanding of how the market works.

Your investment in this book may be one of the most rewarding investment decisions you will ever make. If you follow the principles outlined in this book, you can avoid the timing mistakes made by typical investors, and over a lifetime you can save tens of thousands of dollars in advisory fees. You may find this surprising, but once you understand the principles, you will only need to spend a few hours each year on your investment portfolio.

This book is meant to be a basic primer on how the stock market works and how to invest wisely. You may feel that the deck is stacked against the small investor when it comes to investing, but actually, nothing could be further from the truth. In fact, the deck is stacked against the pros who have hundreds of millions of dollars to invest and are trying to beat the market.

They have huge salary and overhead costs that you can avoid. These professionals do not want you to know this fact because they make their living selling you advice and picking stocks for you; they *need* to make their yacht payments.

This book is written to give the small investor the knowledge I have gained over a lifetime of investing, reading about markets, helping others with their investments, chairing an investment committee at a major investment company, and teaching investment at the college level. This book is the accumulation of the best advice I have found over a lifetime of learning. I am going to provide you with the knowledge that has cost me tens of thousands of dollars in tuition payments and thousands of hours of reading and thinking about investment issues. It is somewhat embarrassing to admit that all of my time, effort, and money can be boiled down to a few simple rules that will allow you to be a savvy investor.

The world of investing can be a terrifying jungle of contradictory advice and incomprehensible jargon. If you walk into this financial jungle and buy stocks on your own, you soon realize you are competing with Wall Street professionals, and if you want to beat the market by selecting stocks, you must beat the professionals who are trained to evaluate stocks. You can try to level the playing field by turning to a professional investment advisor for help, yet most individuals who turn to advisors are dissatisfied with their returns. Financial advisors[1] promise returns above the average market return. After all, who would pay an advisor who states, "All you will earn with me is the average market return"? Over the long run, however, these promises are rarely, if ever, fulfilled.

Although the theories behind investment can be very complicated, the individual investor does not need to understand these theories to outperform the return one expects from the experts. I will explain everything you need to know to eliminate the fees charged by the professional investment advisors. I will show you how to be a savvy investor without earning a PhD in finance. The most excellent news is that you can be an exceptional investor and spend only a few hours each year on your investment portfolio. It may sound too good to be true, but I am convinced that any individual who follows the advice in this book can earn a higher return than the vast majority of individuals who invest in the stock market.

RETIREMENT SAVINGS

Another reason I am writing this book is my concern about the retirement plans of individuals who are currently in the workforce. In most cases today, retirement money goes into defined-contribution (DC) retirement plans.[2] In recent history, retirement plans offered by employers were defined-benefit (DB) plans, which meant the employer made the investment decisions and guaranteed the monthly income at retirement. This is the kind of retirement account your parents or grand-parents probably had. It is unusual for employers today to offer DB plans to their employees. The more common DC retire-ment plans have employees and their employer put money aside for retirement in a retirement account (e.g., a 401k or 403b). This requires employees to decide where this money will be invested. In most cases, employees are not trained to make these crucial investment decisions.

Beyond Social Security, the future of which is uncertain, a retirement investment account should be the backbone of any rational retirement plan. The major part of the funds most employees will have at retirement will be the monies in their retirement accounts. The value of these accounts at retirement will depend critically on the amount of money set aside, when the money is set aside, and the investment decisions made. My fear is that individuals will make investment decisions that could unnecessarily cost them tens of thousands of dollars at retirement. One of the goals of this book is to give you, the reader, the information necessary to make informed investment decisions for retirement.

DETAILS WILL BE REVEALED ABOUT HOW TO INVEST

One of the more frustrating things I have found when reading investment books is that they often do not tell you how to implement the strategies that have been put forward in the book. I promise this book will not suffer from this flaw. If you want to follow the investment tactics advocated in this book, I will give you specific instructions on how to invest. The good news is you do not need a lot of money to become a savvy investor. In fact, this book provides individual investors who have as little as $1,000 to invest with the information necessary to beat all or most of the experts (after all fees are paid). Playing the stock market game intelligently will allow you to be a long-run winner in the stock market.

Although the details of investing can be extremely complicated, as my students can attest, the facts remain that you can spend very little time working on your portfolio and still produce an average return that most money managers would envy. One of the goals of this book is to give you the knowledge that will allow you to invest in the stock market without any external advisors. There may be times, however, when a financial situation becomes so complex that you really should seek the advice of an expert. One example might be when your estate is valued at over $11 million, and you need to try to minimize estate taxes. It is important that you receive advice from a person who has a *fiduciary* responsibility to you; by law, fiduciaries must put your interests above their own. A broker, on the other hand, only has to sell you a "suitable" (a legal term) product and may be motivated to sell you a particular product from which he or she will make the largest commission. This topic will be covered in more detail in Chapter 2.

ABOUT THE AUTHOR

I am a lifelong investor in the stock market. I made my first investment in the market when I was a nineteen-year-old undergraduate student, and I have been invested in the stock market ever since. During the early years, when I made investment decisions, I made the usual mistakes of first-time investors. All I was sure of was that I wanted to be in the stock market. Part of the reason I wrote this book is to help other investors avoid the mistakes I made when I first started investing. I did not start as a savvy investor.

Since the time I made my first investment in the stock market, I have received a PhD in economics and have taught investments at the university level. I have given advice on television, radio, and in print about how individual investors should allocate investment money to maximize their returns. I am currently a professor of economics and management at DePauw University. In the corporate world, I chair an investment committee that oversees the investment of billions of dollars in scores of mutual funds. I have conducted investment seminars for individual investors and have helped individuals construct investment portfolios. Working in academic, corporate, and private sectors gives me a perspective different from most individual investors and investment advisors. Prior to joining the DePauw faculty, I worked as a financial analyst for General Electric Co. in Syracuse, New York.

I have nothing to sell but the knowledge I have accumulated over my lifetime; all investors should require the same from any financial advisor they might hire (i.e., that the advisor does not make a living selling a particular product, but instead makes a living selling you the best advice they can give).

STEPS TO BECOME A SAVVY INVESTOR

Chapter 1 covers a financial checkup. These checkups should be undertaken by all individuals to get their financial house in order before investing in the market. It is important that you review these items before starting the walk down Wall Street.

Chapter 2 focuses on the investment concepts that are important for any investor to understand. College textbooks with hundreds of pages cover many investment concepts. Most of these concepts are irrelevant to the average investor. My goal is to cover just enough of these concepts to help you become a wise investor.

Chapter 3 takes a *brief* look at Social Security. Covering Social Security in depth would require a book ten times longer than this one, and it still would not cover all the subtleties. The one thing I can state with assurance is that Social Security will change over time. Since Social Security is an important part of many people's net worth, I will give an overview of where Social Security is in 2016. Where it will be in 2021, I have no idea, and neither does anyone else.

Chapter 4 covers the essential elements of the stock market, outlining why an investor who has very little to invest can beat the pros in the market. I will try to convince you that the market is basically efficient and tell you how you can use this fact to your advantage.

Chapter 5 reveals the rules you need to follow to earn a higher return than most who use professional money managers. Follow these rules, and you should have a very competitive long-run rate of return. Ignore these rules at the peril of your net worth. (Spoiler alert! There are only two rules: Keep costs low, and allocate your money wisely between risky and less-risky assets.)

Chapter 6 provides specific instructions about how to implement the investment strategies that are advanced in this book. These investment strategies range from the very simple to the more complex. The simplest should not take more than ten minutes a year, and the most complex should not take more than a couple of hours each year. In each case, the average return you earn should beat the average of professional investors.

It is time to get out your pencil and notebook, put on your thinking cap, and get ready to learn how to become a savvy investor. Class begins now!

CHAPTER 1

A FINANCIAL CHECKUP

Before you start investing your hard-earned money in the stock market, you should review a few nitty-gritty items. Most of you reading this book have probably already examined the items covered in this chapter as part of your financial planning, but it is never a bad idea to review your financial position again before adding to or starting any new investment program.

CREDIT CARDS

Credit cards: What would we do without them? They make shopping at a store more convenient and are essential when shopping online. Besides making life simpler, most credit cards today carry reward features that can be intoxicating. I have friends who spend an inordinate amount of time trying to find the best rewards available.

The most important thing to think about when using a credit card is not the reward feature but the payment obligation: Always pay the *entire* balance due every month. If you do not, you will be charged an interest rate as high as 20% or more on your outstanding balance. You should only use your credit card to buy items you can pay for at the end of the month (i.e., as a convenient alternative to carrying cash). If you have a cash flow problem and must charge something you cannot pay for at the end of the month, realize that you are paying a very high premium for the item(s) you bought. In addition, you will be charged interest on *all other items* you bought that month—and every month thereafter—until you pay the total outstanding balance. If you only pay the minimum balance due each month, it can take years to pay off the original purchase and will cost you significantly more than the original purchase price.

Prior to investing in the stock market, one of your first priorities should be to pay off any credit card balances you might have. It is unlikely that the interest rate on a credit card balance will be offset by stock market earnings; hence, it is financially wise to pay off all credit card debt as soon as possible. You will receive a better implicit return on your money by paying off credit card debt than you would if you invested that money in the stock market. It is important to emphasize that you should also refrain from using your credit card when you are carrying a balance from previous months; in most cases, any charges you make during the month will carry an interest charge from the time you make the purchase. One of your first financial priorities should be to pay off all credit card debt as fast as you can and resolve never to carry a card balance past the due date.

INSURANCE

The correct amount and type of insurance you should carry varies from individual to individual, but the theory is quite straightforward: Buy insurance to cover a catastrophic event that you cannot afford to have happen but that also has a low probability of occurring. For example, when you are contemplating what medical insurance to buy, do not buy a policy that will cover small amounts you can easily pay for out-of-pocket. The medical insurance that covers ordinary doctor visits will be very expensive because the insurance company will have many claims and must cover these costs *plus* the cost of processing the claims.

What you should cover with health insurance is a major medical event that could cost tens of thousands of dollars and has a low probability of occurring. The good news is that this high-deductible insurance is often the least expensive because the probability of a catastrophic event occurring is small. A high-deductible health insurance policy is essential for everyone because disastrous events can happen to anyone.

In the United States today, there is no excuse for not having health insurance, given the Affordable Health Care Act that was passed by Congress. If you are covered by a high-deductible health insurance plan at work, you could be eligible for a health savings account (HSA). Check to see if you are eligible for one; there are tax advantages that accrue to a HSA.

When making a decision about car insurance, choose one with the highest deductibles for collision and comprehensive that you can afford to pay. The higher the deductible, the more you will save on car insurance premiums. If you are a good driver, you will not need the collision and comprehensive part of insurance very often, and you will save money in the long-run. If you choose a low deductible and are a good driver, you are essentially paying to have bad drivers' cars fixed. I am sure they appreciate your contribution.

No worries, the good drivers will pay for the repairs.

Liability auto insurance pays a third party if you are judged to be at fault in an automobile accident. The settlements in horrific accidents can be hundreds of thousands of dollars. A payout of this size can wipe out a lifetime of savings for most individuals. States require you to have a minimum liability insurance policy to operate a vehicle in the state; in most cases, you should have substantially more than state minimums. Most financial advisors recommend that you have at least a 250/500/100 liability policy on your car(s).

- The first number represents the limit in thousands (i.e., $250,000) the insurance company will pay one individual who has been injured as result of an accident that is considered your fault.
- The second number represents the most they will pay in total to *all* individuals for one accident that was judged your fault (i.e., $500,000).
- The last number represents the most an insurance company will pay for property damage that was deemed to be your fault (i.e., $100,000).

This high-liability limit is a perfect example of what insurance is designed to do: cover a terrible event that has a low probability of occurring.

For those of you who have acquired a substantial net worth, consider an umbrella policy of at least $1 to $5 million. An umbrella policy kicks in when the limits on your underlying car insurance or homeowner's insurance have been exhausted. This type of insurance is cheap because the probability of such a terrible event occurring is very small. With an umbrella policy of this size, you should be able to sleep well at night knowing that you are covered for most catastrophic events in which you might be held financially liable.

If you are a homeowner, the same kind of analysis should be performed for your homeowner's insurance. Like the previous analysis, you should have high deductibles for losses from fire, theft, etc., and high limits on your homeowner's liability insurance. It is also very important to talk to your insurance agent about what kinds of losses are *not* covered under your homeowner's insurance policy. Water damage from floods and earth movement (earthquakes) are typical examples of items that are not covered—even by an "all-inclusive" homeowner's insurance plan. Although I live in Indiana, I have earth movement insurance because someday soon in geologic time (i.e., the next few hundred years), there will be a major earthquake that will shake Indiana. Major devastation could occur in the area, but there is a low probability of such an event occurring in any particular year. This is, of course, the perfect storm (pun intended) for an insurance policy: shattering loss with a low probability that the event will occur. You should also check to see if your house is in an area that is susceptible to water damage from flooding. If so, you will need to consider adding a flood protection policy. Protecting yourself from devastating loss to your home is essential before beginning any investment program.

Life insurance is another insurance you should consider before you start down the investment road. Like all insurance, you can have too much—as well as too little—life insurance. You need to consider what assets and liabilities you will leave behind if you should die unexpectedly. If you are the sole provider for a family with two small children and have a home mortgage and few assets, you will need much more life insurance than someone who is retired and has a substantial estate with no liabilities. The good news is that in most cases, a decreasing term policy, which offers the highest initial amount of life insurance, will be the correct policy for most families. For example, with a twenty-year decreasing term life insurance policy (there are also policies with terms of twenty-five or thirty years), the premium you pay stays the same over the twenty years that the policy is in force, but the amount of coverage decreases until the insurance reaches zero after twenty years. This kind of policy is appropriate in the majority of cases because as your assets grow and your liabilities decrease (e.g., your mortgage declines, your retirement account grows, and your children leave home), your need for life insurance also declines. Decreasing term life insurance policies offer maximum protection for a given premium during the first years when you usually need the most coverage. For most individuals, this is an instance where cheaper is better.

When determining the correct amount of life insurance to purchase initially, try to imagine how much money it would take for your family to maintain their current lifestyle, coupled with any future needs they may have (e.g., college expenses). Try to imagine what a typical family budget might look like in the future, what sources of income they might have, and what expenses they might encounter. Take the annual deficit from this budget and multiply it by twenty to give you a very rough starting point for the amount of life insurance you might need to purchase. This should allow your family to draw 5% per year from this insurance settlement and live the life they had before your death. Be sure to check to see if you are covered by a life insurance policy provided by your employer and subtract that from the amount you think you should purchase. If you are single with no dependents or retired with a large estate, the correct amount for life insurance may be zero; however, if you are the sole breadwinner in a family with several dependents, the amount might be quite large.

Long-term disability insurance is another insurance you should evaluate before you start investing in the stock market.

Most families have some form of life insurance; disability insurance is much less likely to be part of a current financial plan. If you are forty years old, unless you have a family history of early death, you are statistically more likely to become disabled than you are to die. Young families face a far greater risk of family insolvency from a disabling injury than from premature death. The facts of disability are:

- Just over 1 in 4 of today's twenty-year-olds will become disabled before they retire.
- Accidents are *not* usually the culprit. Instead, back injuries, cancer, heart disease, and other illnesses cause the majority of long-term absences.[3]

There are basically two kinds of disability insurance: short-term and long-term. It is important that you are covered by some type of long-term disability—either through work or through a private policy. It is also important to have a basic understanding of what Social Security will cover. Warning: Understanding Social Security disability insurance will not be easy. A good place to start your research is the book *Get What's Yours* by Kotlikoff, Moeller, and Solman.

In summary, insurance is simply a way of transferring risk from the insured to the insurance company. You give up a set amount of money—the premium—and in return, the insurance company will pay you an amount of money if something calamitous happens. Simply stated, insurance is a way to mitigate risk. You trade certainty (i.e., a premium that must be paid) for the uncertainty that your house might burn down. No one buys auto insurance because they hope to crash their car or home insurance because they hope their house will be blown away in a tornado. Insurance exists to provide you with peace of mind, knowing that a shattering event that has a low probability of occurring will not create financial devastation for your family.

RAINY DAY MONEY

Everyone should have a rainy day account set up for any financial emergencies. This rainy day fund can protect you from a disruption of your income stream or any unexpected expenses that could arise. The stock market is absolutely *not* the place to have rainy day money invested. For example, it would be possible for your car to break down, requiring a major expenditure at the same time the stock market is down 20%, forcing you to sell your investments at a low point in the market.

A good rule of thumb is that the money you have invested in the stock market should not be needed for the next five years. A five-year window will give your portfolio time to recover from any major downturn in the stock market. Rainy day money needs to be in a financial instrument that has a stable value (e.g., a savings account).

The $64,000 question is how much should be set aside in a rainy day account. A starting point is to have six months of expenses saved in this kind of account. For some, this will be more than is necessary, but for others, this sum of money could be insufficient. If you and your spouse both have jobs at companies that are financially stable, you might not need six months' savings in a rainy day account, but if you are the sole provider for a family and are employed in an industry that has cyclical fluctuations, you might need more than six months of expenses in the fund. Take a realistic look at your current situation and decide the appropriate amount to set aside in your rainy day account. The purpose of the fund is to keep you from having to sell stock at the worse possible moment.

Rainy day money should be invested in a stable-value, completely safe asset that pays a competitive interest rate. Money market mutual funds historically had some of the highest interest rates available; today, however, it is banks that appear to have the best rates for short-term investments. Currently, money market mutual funds not only pay lower interest rates than savings accounts; they are also going through some major regulatory revisions. It is not clear what money market mutual funds will look like after these revisions are implemented. At this point in time, it better to have your rainy day money is a savings account at a bank.

One way to do your due diligence in finding a suitable rainy day account is to Google the term "high-interest savings accounts." My students are sure Google is *the* source of all useful information, and I have to admit I also use it. Make sure the account you open is FDIC insured; remember, this money is your safe money, and you do not want to take any risks with it. It is also important to understand any fees the bank will charge for this account and how convenient it will be to access your money. After some research, you may decide that your current bank offers a competitive interest rate, and the convenience of having everything under one roof is worth any loss of return.

A legitimate question to ask at this point is whether a certificate of deposit (CD) at a bank might be a place to park your rainy day money. A CD requires the saver to commit to leaving money at the bank for a specific period. Remember, rainy day money needs a parking area (easy in and easy out) for money you might need *immediately*; this is not an area where you are trying to eke out any excess returns. In most cases, the extra return is not worth tying up your money for any period of time. With rainy day money, play it safe.

RETIREMENT INCOME

Not too far in the distant past, many individuals could count on three sources of income when it was time to retire: a company pension, Social Security, and personal savings.

This three-legged stool has changed dramatically in recent years. In most cases, the company pension (or defined-benefit (DB) plan) is no longer being offered. Even if your company has a DB plan, there is a possibility the company is underfunding the plan—just ask the city employees of Detroit. It is also possible that the company will go bankrupt before you retire. Although there are safeguards for these kinds of events, they add uncertainty to any retirement plan. In general, most future retirees will not be able to count on having a DB plan for retirement.

The second source of income a retiree could count on in retirement was Social Security. The problems with Social Security are well documented, primarily that the projected outflows exceed the inflows of money.[4] It is clear that the current structure of Social Security is not sustainable. Some combination of raising the Social Security tax and/or reducing benefits will eventually be required. Even in the 1930s, the architects of Social Security knew they were creating a system that was not sustainable—at least, not in the form they were designing. During the original debate to create Social Security, one senator told colleagues not to worry about the long-term problems of Social Security because when those problems manifest themselves, "We will be dead." They are all now dead, and we have inherited the problems.

> The effort to shift benefits to early participants in the program and away from later participants was done for economic, distributional, and political reasons. Under the Act of 1935, Social Security benefits in the early years were projected, in many cases, to be quite low— often below amounts payable under some state old-age assistance programs. In addition, concerns about the overall economy in 1939 (which had slipped back into recession between 1937 and 1938) no doubt made policymakers reluctant to limit domestic spending (or to implement scheduled tax increases). Finally, there was probably substantial political appeal to shifting benefits

to the early years (and postponing tax increases). In any event, this approach and, perhaps more importantly, other changes made later created a situation in which Social Security was a very good deal for participants in the start-up phase of the program but less so for future retirees.[5]

The first monthly Social Security payment was issued on January 31, 1940, to Ida May Fuller of Ludlow, Vermont.[6] From 1937–39, she paid a total of $24.75 into the Social Security system. Her first check was for $22.54. After her second check, Fuller had already received more than she had contributed over the three-year period. She ultimately reached her one hundredth birthday, dying in 1975, and had collected a total of $22,888.92.

The current pay-as-you-go system created big winners, and as with any zero-sum game, if there are big winners, there must be big losers (i.e., many of the current workers). In my public finance class, we spend several days discussing Social Security. Since I first began teaching the course, I have told all my students in the class to assume that Social Security will not be there when they retire. If Social Security is still paying benefits when they retire, they can think of those benefits as manna from heaven.

The only reason I am nice to you is that I want you to pay my Social Security.

While we cannot be sure about the future of Social Security, we *can* be sure that changes are required for the system to stay afloat. The baby boomers are starting to retire, which means they are no longer paying into the system but are taking money *out* of the system. This means less money is flowing in, and more money is flowing out. This negative cash flow phenomenon will continue for the near future. Current projections are that the Social Security Trust Fund will exhaust all reserves by the mid-2030s.[7] Although the outlook for Social Security can be quite negative, one is reminded of what President Franklin Roosevelt said about Social Security: "With these taxes [i.e., Social Security payroll tax] in there, no damn politician can ever scrap my Social Security program."[8] The implication of the Social Security tax is that it establishes a contract between you (the taxpayer) and the federal government so that when you retire, you will be able to collect Social Security benefits for the rest of your life (i.e., no damn politician can ever scrap your Social Security program.)

This leaves the third source of retirement income, personal savings, as the most important contributor to retirement income for most individuals. As I stated in the Introduction, this is why the information contained in this book is so important. Simply put, your retirement income will depend critically on the investment decisions you make while you are employed. Reliance on personal savings and investment decisions made by individuals for retirement income is a daring experiment being undertaken in the US, and it could have profound effects for future retirees. No longer can individuals rely on the government or on corporations for the majority of their retirement income. Individuals are not only responsible for how much to save but also for how to invest those dollars for retirement. Do it in a smart way, and you can accumulate a very nice nest egg. Save too little or invest in the wrong things, and you could be facing disaster when you retire. This book is designed to make you a savvy investor, thus tilting the odds that you will have more net worth at retirement than you would have if you had not read this book.

RETIREMENT AND YOUR FAVORITE UNCLE SAM

When thinking about saving for retirement, one of the first things you should do is find out the details of your employer's retirement program. Most companies today will have a 403(b) or 401(k) plan (i.e., a defined-contribution (DC) plan). In many cases, companies will have some kind of match for the dollars you put into your retirement account. This means the company will add dollars to your retirement account if you contribute to the retirement account. An important element to note is that these plans are funded with pretax dollars, which means the dollars put into these accounts are not taxed in the year you set aside the money. Each year, this will reduce your federal income tax by the amount you set aside, multiplied by your federal marginal tax rate (the federal income tax rate on the last dollar you earned).[9]

For example, assume you are in the 25% marginal tax bracket and decide to set aside $100 per month for retirement. If the company you work for matches dollar-for-dollar what you set aside, your account would have $200 each month, and it would only cost you $75 out-of-pocket. Why did it not cost $100 out-of-pocket? You have a generous Uncle Sam who will not tax your income if you put the money into a qualified retirement account, meaning the $100 you earned today will not be taxed today. This saves you $25 (100 X 0.25) in taxes for the year you put the money in the account. You will later have to pay taxes on money *withdrawn* from this account, but even if you have to pay the $25 in taxes at a later date, your Uncle Sam has still floated you an interest-free loan—and allowed you to earn a financial return on *his* money.

The bottom line is that for $75 out-of-pocket, you have $200 in your retirement account.

Uncle Sam: I am offering you a thirty-year interest-free loan.

One way to postpone federal—and possibly state income tax—collection is to establish one of the several types of retirement accounts for which the federal government allows individuals to set aside money for retirement and earn tax-deferred returns. In addition to previously mentioned 401(k) and 403(b) accounts, there are Individual Retirement Accounts (IRAs), Roth IRAs, and Self-Employed Plans (SEPs). All of these plans, except the Roth IRAs, allow individuals to set aside money today and not pay current federal income tax on the money saved.

A well-balanced strategy of 80% equities (stocks) and 20% fixed-income debt instruments (corporate bonds) has earned approximately 13% per year over the past forty years.[10] There are, of course, no guarantees that the future returns will be the same as they have been in the past. As a starting point, it might be reasonable to assume that a 10% annual return could be earned by a portfolio of at least 80% equities and 20% fixed-income instruments.

If you are in the 25% marginal tax bracket, set aside $500 a month in one of the tax-deferred plans for forty years, and earn 10% per year, then the $180,000 (i.e., $500 X 480 X 0.75 [due to tax savings]) out-of-pocket you will have invested will turn into $3,188,390. If you have an employer who will match your contributions, you will have $6,376,780 (see chart below).

Albert Einstein reportedly once said, that "Compound interest is the eighth wonder of the world. He who understands it, earns it. He who doesn't, pays it." The bad news is you will have to pay income tax when you withdraw the money from you retirement account.

Chart 1

The magic of compounding.

Assuming a 10% rate of return:

Number of years	Gross per month contribution	Net contribution 25% tax bracket	Terminal value without match	Terminal value with 100% match
10	$500	$45,000	$103,276	$206,552
20	$500	$90,000	$382,848	$765,697
30	$500	$135,000	$1,139,663	2,279,325
40	$500	$180,000	$3,188,390	$6,376,780

The big takeaway from the above chart is that the earlier you start saving, the more the magic of compounding can work. Moving from saving for ten years to forty years (i.e., four times longer and four times more invested) causes your terminal value to increase by more than thirty times!

If you take the same pretax $500 and put the after-tax $375 (i.e., 500 X 0.75) amount into a taxable account that has an after-tax return of 7.5% (i.e., 10% X 0.75), after forty years you would have $1,141,020 (see Chart 2) instead of the $3,188,390 shown above in Chart 1. Of course, you won't have paid any taxes on the $3,188,390. Assuming, however, that you take this money out at a 25% tax rate, you will still have $2,391,292, which is 109% more money! If you can get an employer's match, you will have $4,782,585—more than *four times* what you would in a taxable account.

Chart 2
Assuming a $500 ($375 after taxes) per month investment, a 10% before-tax return, and a 25% marginal tax rate:

Number of years	Value in taxable account, $375 per month, and 7.5% return	Value in retirement account after tax—Chart 1, column 4 above X 0.75	Value in retirement account after tax with 100% employer match, Chart 1, column 5 above X 0.75
10	$67,141	$77,457	$154,914
20	$208,947	$287,136	$574,272
30	$508,450	$854,747	$1,709,494
40	$1,141,020	$2,391,292	$4,782,585

The above charts illustrate the power of compounding and also show the gains you receive by deferring your tax obligations. Not only do you receive an *interest-free loan* (because you can defer your taxes) but you can also *earn a return* on this deferred tax payment. Thank you, Uncle Sam!

Of course, the above results are dependent on your marginal tax bracket and the rate of return you earn. The higher your marginal tax bracket, the more valuable this kind of deduction becomes. Also, the rate of return you earn will have a profound effect on the total dollars in your account. The underlying assumption in the above example is that you will be in the same tax bracket when you retire as you were when you put the money in the retirement account. The amount of federal tax you have to pay on the retirement account will depend on the marginal tax bracket you are in when you withdraw the funds. You could, of course, be in a higher bracket; or you could be in a lower bracket. As the above example shows, the fact that you essentially receive an interest-free loan and can earn a return on that loan can make a substantial difference in the final value of your retirement account. The moral to the story: You should put as much as you can afford, up to the statutory limit, into a tax-deferred retirement account, *especially when you have a match from your employer.*

An important footnote to the above discussion is that there is a 10% tax penalty if you withdraw money from this account before you reach the age of 59½. The IRS will waive that penalty in some cases, but you should really consider the money locked away for retirement. If you have set up a rainy day account, you should not have to tap into your retirement account before you retire. A mistake many individuals make is cashing in these accounts when they change jobs. Instead, let the accounts continue to do the magic of compounding.

TRADITIONAL/ROTH IRAS

If you are eligible for a retirement plan at work and want to also open a traditional IRA or Roth IRA, certain income restrictions apply. As of 2015, your income must be below

$98,000 for a full deduction from your federal income tax. If you are eligible to open an IRA and are currently in a low marginal tax bracket, it may make sense to establish a Roth IRA. The major difference between a traditional IRA and a Roth IRA is *when* you pay the federal income taxes. With a traditional IRA, the monies you put into an IRA are pretax investments; you pay taxes when you *withdraw* money from the traditional IRA. Roth IRAs, on the other hand, are funded with after-tax dollars. This means that since you have already paid federal income tax on the money you deposited into the account, when you withdraw the money from a Roth IRA, it is not subject to federal income tax—including all gains in that account. In order to withdraw your earnings tax-penalty-free from a Roth IRA, you must be older than 59½, and your initial contribution must have been made to your Roth IRA five years before the date when you start withdrawing funds.

One of the advantages of a Roth IRA is that there are no lifetime minimum distribution requirements during the owner's lifetime. You can start withdrawing money from a Roth IRA after age 59½ as you deem appropriate. In a traditional IRA, there are minimum distribution requirements after you reach the age of 70½. Since you have paid no income tax on the money in a traditional IRA, the federal government wants its share of your money. The IRS requires that at age 70½, individuals make at least a minimum distribution from an IRA based on actuarial tables. The money withdrawn from the traditional IRA will be subject to federal and state income taxes.

The answer to the question of which IRA is best for you is not easy. Fortunately, there are free programs available on the Internet that will help you analyze which IRA is best for your particular circumstances.

401(k), 403(b)

In today's business environment, most firms have either a 401(k) or a 403(b) retirement plan available for their employees. 401(k) plans are offered by for-profit companies, and 403(b) plans are offered by nonprofit companies. Since the main difference between these two retirement plans is what type of organization you work for, this book will treat them as equivalent.

The two main advantages of these retirement programs—401(k) and 403(b)—are the tax deferral and the company match that is available from most employers. If your employer has some kind of match, it is important to take advantage of this "free" money offer. This match money comes close to being the illusive "free lunch." The catch is that in most cases, you cannot touch the money without penalty until you are age 59½. But the potential value of this account at retirement is well worth the wait.

The maximum you can contribute to these plans is tied to a cost-of-living formula; hence, the limits will change over time. In 2015, the limits for annual contributions to 401(k) and 403(b) accounts were $18,000, with a catch-up contribution limit of $6,000 for employees aged fifty and older. If you started contributing when you were twenty-two, retired when you were sixty-six, contributed the maximum $18,000 each year, and earned 10% per year, then you would accumulate over $14 million in your retirement account. Oh, to be young and have the ability to set aside $18,000 a year for forty-four years! The bad news is that you will have to pay taxes on the $14 million, but I doubt you will find many people who will feel sorry for you. This $14 million should be enough for most people to have a very comfortable retirement.

The main consideration now becomes where you should invest your annual 401(k) or 403(b) contributions so you can utilize the magic of compounding. As mentioned in the Introduction, one of the main purposes of this book is to help you make wise investment choices so that you will have a substantial nest egg when you retire. The takeaway from this section is to start saving early for retirement and thereby earn a high investment return.

SELF-EMPLOYED PLANS

All self-employed individuals—from doctors, lawyers, and real estate brokers to dog walkers—can set up self-employed plans (SEP). In 2015, you could invest up to 25% of up to $212,000 of employment income, or $53,000 ($212,000 X 0.25), in your SEP account. SEPs work in a fashion similar to traditional IRA, 403(b), and 401(k) accounts in that dollars invested in the account are not taxed until they are withdrawn at retirement. Like all of the above, this is a self-directed plan that requires you to choose where to invest your money. Once again, the goal of this book is to show you how to maximize the return on your investments.

An interesting question to ask is why the maximum limits on these retirement plans are so different, varying from $5,500 for a traditional IRA to $53,000 for a SEP. I believe it has something to do with the individuals who use these accounts. In general, lower-income individuals use a traditional IRA, and more wealthy individuals use an SEP. Why do I think you are not surprised about the rich getting a better break?

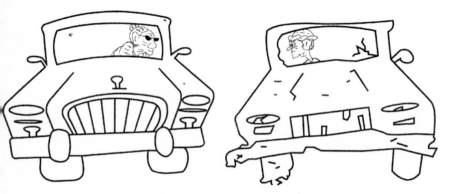

I invested in the same stocks you did.
The only difference is I did it in a taxable account.

COLLEGE SAVINGS 101, OR "IS IT 529?"

A provision in the tax code, section 529, allows individuals to set up college savings plans or prepaid tuition plans for anyone designated as a beneficiary. In most cases, this will be a child or grandchild, but the designated person does not have to be a relative. There is no limit to the number of plans you can set up. These plans are operated by states and educational institutions and offer tax advantages and other incentives to make it easier to save for college or other post-secondary training.

The biggest draw of 529 plans is the tax benefits that come with these accounts. Many states let you deduct your 529 plan contributions on your state income tax return (up to the state's limit). The earnings on this account will be deferred from federal income taxes and never will be collected if the money is withdrawn for qualified higher-education expenses such as tuition, fees, book, room, board, and computer technology. This means that the magical compounding effect will never be taxed *if* the money is used for qualified educational expenses. Of course, the longer a 529 exists, the more tax-free compounding money will be in the account. If you are going to establish a 529 account, start as early as possible.

You do not have to live in the state where you establish the 529 plan, and your beneficiary, in most cases, is not restricted to going to school in that state. Your first research assignment should be to look at the state where you live, because the state may have incentives for residents of the state. For example, Indiana taxpayers are eligible for a state income tax credit of 20% of contributions to their 529 accounts up to a $1,000 credit per year (thank you, Indiana). This means that if you live in Indiana, you can set aside $5,000 per year in a 529, and it will save you $1,000 in state income taxes (if you itemize deductions on your federal return, you will have an increase in taxes at the federal level because of the reduction in taxes paid to the state). The state you live in may also have incentives for residents, so you need to check the current incentives where you reside. If your state does not offer any incentives, then you can base your decision on the return and expenses of the various states' programs.

As previously stated, the main benefit of a 529 is that the earnings will never be taxed if used for a qualified expenditure. The result is that all earnings go toward college expenses—not some proportion of the earnings to the federal and state governments. Another advantage of these plans is that your plan always stays under your control and is not accessible to the beneficiary unless you say so, no matter what the beneficiary's age. It is a flexible tool with low minimum and high maximum contributions that can be redirected to another beneficiary if the original beneficiary does not need the money.

Of course, there is a catch to 529s. (Or is it a catch-22?) If you take money out of a 529 for a purpose other than college expenses, you risk paying income tax on the gain *and* a 10% penalty. Even with the catch, however, it remains an excellent way to save for college expenses.

RENT OR BUY

The choice between renting or buying a home is among the biggest financial decisions most individuals will ever make. The federal tax laws, which offer substantial tax breaks for homeowners, are written to encourage individuals to buy homes. Assuming you itemize your deductions, two of the major expenses of owning a home are deductible from your federal income taxes: interest expense on your mortgage and the property tax on the home. The payment a renter makes has an embedded interest and property tax charge that is paid by the landlord but is not deductible on the renter's federal tax return. Also, if you sell your primary home, any realized gains are not taxed—up to $500,000 for a married couple and $250,000 for a single tax filer—as long as you have lived in the house for at least twenty-four months in the five years prior to the sale of the house. Both of these provisions in the tax code can have profound effects on one's financial position. Uncle Sam wants you to buy a home. Since interest payments and property taxes are deductions from income, the higher the marginal tax bracket you are in, the more valuable these deductions are. If you are in the 35% tax bracket, each dollar you can deduct saves you thirty-five cents in income tax, whereas if you are in the 20% tax bracket, you only save twenty cents on each dollar you deduct.

There are many factors to consider when making a decision on renting or buying a home. Some of the more important factors include current home prices, how long you plan to stay in the area, current mortgage interest rates, the cost of maintaining your home, and the future of housing prices in the area.

In almost all cases, if you want to sell $250,000 of stock, you can complete the sale in a fraction of a second, and the expenses related to selling are minimal—substantially less than

1%. In the housing market, however, selling and closing costs can be substantial. Also, it can take weeks or months to find a buyer who is willing to purchase your house. This potential illiquidity of a house (i.e., the amount of time it takes from listing your house until you receive the money from the sale) is another factor you should consider when you make the buy-or-rent decision.

It is intuitively obvious to the most casual observer (confession: I used to use the same expression in a math proof when I had no idea what I was doing) that the decision to buy versus rent is a complex decision. The Internet has software that can help you make the buy-or-rent decision, but while the software can help make the decision, it is still a leap of faith to buy your first house.

You need to think of buying a home as you would a consumption item—like buying a car—not an investment decision. We have all heard of tremendous gains on houses, such as a house bought for $50,000 that sells thirty years later for $300,000. This $250,000 profit sounds like a real bonanza. One needs to consider, however, all the home expenses: closing costs at the time of purchase, interest expenses over thirty years, property taxes, insurance, maintenance, improvement, selling costs, etc. Often, when talking about how much money a person makes in the real estate market, one disregards these additional costs.

One must also consider the impact of inflation on the initial purchase price. The price of a home would have to increase just to keep up with inflation. The bottom line is that the average annual home price increase for the US during the period 1900–2012 was only 3.1% per year, just a shade better than the inflation rate of 3.0% per year.[11] This 0.1% real return is not a ringing endorsement of investing in housing.

GOLD AND OTHER COLLECTIBLES

If you enjoy collecting fine art, stamps, or any other collectibles, then by all means do it—but do it as a hobby, not as an investment. If you make money buying and selling collectibles, think of it as manna from heaven. Collectibles are barren assets that do not pay dividends or generate interest income. In many cases, you may have to pay storage and insurance costs for your valuable collectibles. When my son Mark was young, he collected baseball cards. Mark could tell me the "market value" of scores of baseball cards and was always buying cards (with my money) at less than "market value." When he would show me a card and tell me how much money he had made by buying low, I would do my *Jerry Maguire* imitation and say, "Show me the money!" Mark was having fun, and I was having fun watching him have fun. But as an investment, it did not work out.

Gold has some very nice properties in manufacturing processes, but most individuals do not buy gold to use for manufacturing. Rather, they buy gold to sell to someone else at a higher price. These buyers are operating under the "greater fool" theory: someone will buy a BIC pen for $50,000 if they think there is a greater fool who will pay $60,000 for it in a month's time. The problem with "greater fool" games is that there is always one fool at the end who is holding a BIC pen he or she paid $60,000 for when the public finally realizes its intrinsic value is only $1. Eventually, the public will realize that the emperor has no clothes, and then the "greater fool" game is over.

There are many famous "bubbles" in history, including the tulip-bulb craze, the South Sea bubble, the dot-com bubble of the late 1990s and early 2000, and the most recent housing bubble. In all of these cases, the product sold for more than its intrinsic value, and eventually, the price came crashing down. If you are playing the gold game, you are betting you can find a greater fool to buy your gold and pay you a higher price in the future. Be careful if you play this game; *you* could be the fool at the end of the game holding a BIC pen—or an ounce of gold.

WILLS AND ADVANCED DIRECTIVES

Wills and advanced directives (such as living wills and powers of attorney) are written, legal instructions regarding your preferences for the distribution of your estate and your preferences for medical care if you are unable to make decisions for yourself. Advanced directives guide choices that doctors and others must make if you are, for example, in a coma or the late stages of dementia and are unable to make your wishes known as to what medical treatment you want or do not want. Advanced directives are not just for older adults; unexpected end-of-life situations can happen at any age. It is important for all adults to have these documents and have them prepared by a lawyer who specializes in these kinds of documents. Although these types of discussions can be uncomfortable, it is important that you discuss what your wishes are with the people who will be making decisions on your behalf. These discussions and documents can be invaluable during trying times.

SUMMARY

It is important to take a look at your financial situation *before* you start any investment program. This chapter has outlined topics you should think about before investing in the stock market. One element you should examine is credit card debt. An investor would have to be really skilled and very lucky to earn a return on stocks that would exceed the interest charges on credit card debt. An investor also needs to protect himself or herself from ruinous losses by buying insurance for life, health, car, disability, home, and a devastating event (i.e., an umbrella policy).

Remember, you can buy too much insurance, as well as too little. Buy insurance for a major loss that has a low probably of occurring. These kinds of policies will protect you from financial ruin.

It is also prudent to set up a rainy day fund, so you have cash for any unexpected expense(s) that might occur. You do not want to be forced to sell stock when the market is down 40% because you need a new car.

Renting vs. owning a home is also something you need to carefully consider. There are some fairly substantial tax incentives for owning a home; selling and buying a home, however, can be expensive. The general rule of thumb is that you need to stay in the same home for at least five years for the purchase to make economic sense.

If you enjoy antique cars or collecting stamps, then I would encourage you to do those things as hobbies. But if you are doing them because you think of them as investment vehicles (pun intended), then you can get severely burned. These markets tend to be very thin, and investors will need to develop some expertise in the commodity they are buying. Always remember the "greater fool" theory.

Lastly, although it is difficult to talk about, all adults need to prepare a last will and testament, as well as certain documents that deal with end-of-life situations. Hire an expert who specializes in these kinds of documents. You do not want your family to find out that the free or low-cost document you downloaded from the Internet is really not what you thought it was and causes major legal problems in a very stressful time.

Once you have competed these warm-up exercises, you are in a position to start an investment program.

CHAPTER 2

THE LANGUAGE OF INVESTING

E very discipline has its own particular language. In this chapter, I will define a few terms that will help you understand "stock market speak." Stock market speak is not only what academics and professionals use; it's also what journalists use in the popular press. I will also explain how you can measure the performance of the stock market. Knowing the performance of the stock market is crucial because it will allow you to judge the performance of your portfolio vis-à-vis the average market return. Being above average is good; being below average is bad. Finally, I will examine why it is important that if you hire an advisor to help with your investments, you hire a fiduciary.

MARKET CAP

Throughout this book and in financial literature, you will see the terms "market capitalization" and "market cap." A market cap, or capitalization, is the current price of the stock multiplied by the number of shares held by the public. Hence, the market cap is the total value the stock market places on a company at a given point in time. For example, if a company has 1,000 shares outstanding, and its current stock price is $10, then the market cap of the company would be $10,000. In July 2015, Apple had the largest market cap in the world at $756 billion; Microsoft had the second-largest market cap at $384 billion.[12] Yes, Apple's market value was almost twice that of the second-largest company, Microsoft.

When considering market capitalization, the stock market is often divided into three categories: large-cap, mid-cap, and small-cap. Although there is no universal definition of where to draw the line between large-cap, mid-cap, and small-cap stocks, the distinction is made so that the large-cap stocks are the 500 largest companies in the US, mid-cap stocks are the next 400 largest companies, and small-cap are the next 600 largest companies. These divisions will become important later in the book because there is evidence that in the long run, small-cap stocks tend to outperform the large-cap stocks.[13] This excess return does not happen every day, week, month, or year, but over long periods of time, small-cap stocks have had a better return than large-cap stocks—even after adjusting for risk. For the investor who wants to play a somewhat "faster game" (with a potentially higher return) than the simplest investment strategy, I will suggest that you tilt (not *plunge*) your portfolio to include more small-cap stocks.

MEASURING MARKET PERFORMANCE

How market performance is measured is a question that seems like it should have an easy answer. Like many seemingly straightforward questions, however, the answer is not always simple. In this case, the answer depends on what is meant by "the market," and that answer is important because it becomes the benchmark by which we judge the success of an investor's investments. If someone states that he made 10% last year, you have no idea if this is good or bad. If "the market" was up 15%, then 10% does not sound very good. If "the market" was down 3%, however, then the person had an excellent year. There are several published indexes of performance you need to understand when you invest in the stock market.

1. THE DOW

One of the most publicized market indicators is the Dow Jones Industrial Average (DJIA), or the Dow. The average was created by the *Wall Street Journal* and was first calculated in 1896. The DJIA is composed of thirty very large, publicly traded "industrial"[14] companies based in the US. The fact that there are only thirty very large companies in the average is one of the Dow's major flaws. This means there are no mid-cap or small-cap stocks in the DJIA. Not all stocks move in lockstep, so it would be possible for these thirty stocks to move up by a certain percentage while the rest of the market moved either up or down by a significantly different percentage. There is no attempt to include a cross section of companies in the Dow. If you are interested in how the thirty largest companies in the US are doing, you might want to look at the Dow, but if your interest is outside these thirty stocks, then you should look elsewhere. A related problem is that these thirty stocks are all "industrial" stocks, so this lack of representation of other types of companies (transportation, utilities, etc.) also contributes to a bias in the reported average.

Another problem with the Dow is the lack of meaning of the number itself. In the beginning, it was meant to be the average price of the thirty stocks in the DJIA. One would simply add the prices of the thirty stocks and divide by thirty. This would allow you to know the average price of a stock in the DJIA. As I write this book, the DJIA is in the 18,000 range. The total current prices of all thirty stocks is less than 18,000, so 18,000 is certainly not the average. To compensate for the effects of stock splits and other adjustments that have been made over time, the thirty stock prices in the DJIA are added together and then divided by 0.1557 (the same as multiplying by 6.42)—not by thirty. The divisor will continue to change with stock splits, etc. Hence, the DJIA conveys no information about the average price of an individual stock in the DJIA.

The DJIA is a price-weighted average. This means that a stock with a higher price will have more influence on the average than a stock with a lower price. To illustrate, assume you create a Lemon Industrial Average (LIA) in the same fashion as the DJIA, with two stocks that have exactly the same market capitalization. Stock A is selling for $100 per share, and stock B is selling for $10.

Stock	Price	Number of shares	Market cap
A	$100	1,000	$100,000
B	$10	10,000	$100,000

If you calculate the LIA: $(100 + 10)/2 = 55$
Suppose stock A increases to $110:

Stock	Price	Number of shares	Market cap
A	$110	1,000	$110,000
B	$10	10,000	$100,000

If you now calculate the new LIA: $(110 + 10)/2 = 60$

$10,000 of market capitalization has been created, and the LIA has increased from 55 to 60.

Now assume a different scenario: The price of stock B increases from $10 to $11.

Stock	Price	Number of shares	Market cap
A	$100	1,000	$100,000
B	$11	10,000	$110,000

Now the LIA is: $(100 + 11)/2 = 55.5$

In both cases, the total market capitalization has increased by $10,000, but in one case, the LIA increased from 55 to 60, while in the other case, it increased from 55 to 55.5. Because the stock that is priced at $100 must increase to $110 in order for a 10% increase to occur—and the stock selling for $10 must only increase to $11 to achieve the same 10% increase in market capitalization—the LIA will send out different signals to the public about how the market is doing *even though the same amount of wealth has been created.* There is absolutely no reason why the higher-priced stock should have more influence on the LIA—or the DJIA.

Although there are numerous problems with the DJIA, it is still widely reported. Why? Because individuals are comfortable with the concept—even though they have no idea how the number is calculated or what it means.

2. S&P 500 (or Standard & Poor's 500)

One of my favorite questions is, how many stocks are there in the S&P 500? When I ask this in class, students are always more wary of answering an obvious question than one that requires a lot of thought; they assume there is a catch. In most cases, they are correct, but in this case the answer is obvious: 500. The S&P 500 is a US-based index. When the S&P 500 is calculated, Standard & Poor's uses market capitalization of 500 of the largest companies in the US. These companies have their common stock listed on the New York Stock Exchange (NYSE) or National Association of Securities Dealers Automated Quotations (NASDAQ, the second-largest stock exchange in the US). Although there are thousands of stocks traded each day that are not part of the S&P 500, the stocks in the S&P 500 make up approximately 80% of the value of trades during a typical day. Unless you are trading primarily in small-cap stocks, this index will give you a much better picture of what the market is doing than the DJIA. Instead of looking at only thirty stocks, you now have a universe of 500 stocks that represent most of the market value traded each day.

The other thing to note about the S&P 500 is that it is an *index*, not an *average*. The index with which most individuals are probably already familiar is the Consumer Price Index (CPI). The CPI measures the change in the total cost of a bundle of goods and services that the typical consumer might purchase. One can imagine the Bureau of Labor Statistics sending individuals out to purchase a basket of goods and services that the Bureau thinks the typical consumer would consume in a month. The next month, they buy the same basket of goods and services and compare the total cost they have paid for the same bundle. For simplicity, assume the bundle costs $100 in an arbitrary base year. If the current CPI is 150, then the same bundle of goods now costs $150. This implies that the typical bundle of goods purchased by the average consumer now costs 50% (150/100) more than it did in the base year.

The S&P 500 uses the same technique to construct its stock index as that used by the CPI. The difference is that rather than calculating the price of consumer goods, the S&P 500 calculates the change in the market capitalization of the 500 largest companies in the US. The base for the S&P 500 is the average market capitalization of 500 large companies in the years 1941–43. The S&P 500 is constructed by adding up the current market capitalization of the 500 companies in the index and dividing that number by the market capitalization in 1941–43.[15] Of course, adjustments to the denominator have been made as new companies are added and old companies are dropped from the index. This quotient (current market cap/base-year market cap) will show an investor how market capitalization of the 500 largest companies has changed over time. This calculation makes sense because it gives an indication of how much wealth has been created.

When an index is calculated, the quotient (current market capitulation/base market capitalization) is multiplied by a base index number. The S&P 500 uses a base index number of 10, instead of the more frequently used 100. If the current S&P 500 index is 20, this would indicate that the total capitalization of these 500 companies has doubled from the base years.

As I write this book, the current S&P Index is 2,037.41, which means the value of the 500 stocks has increased 203.74 times since 1941–43. The implication is that each dollar invested in the S&P 500 in 1941–43 would now be worth $203.74.

Most of the problems with the DJIA have been corrected by the S&P 500. The number of stocks has increased from thirty in the DJIA to 500 in the S&P 500. Although there are thousands of stocks traded each day that are not in the index, most of the absolute dollars that are traded in a day are in one of the S&P 500 stocks. If an investor is wondering what the market is doing and how much market value was generated or lost during the day, then the S&P 500 would provide a better answer than the DJIA.

Any market capitalization-weighted index like the S&P 500 conveys valuable information about what is happening to the market value of stocks, whereas a price-weighted average like the Dow can give a false impression of what is happening in the stock market. To illustrate, a 1% move in the price of a stock that has a large market capitalization will create more wealth than a 1% move in the price of a stock that has a small market capitalization. In 2016, Apple had the largest market capitalization in the US stock market, with almost 4% of the total capitalization of the 500 stocks in the S&P 500 index.

On the other hand, if each of the 500 stocks had an equal weight, each stock would have 1/5 of 1% influence on the index. With Apple's almost 4% weight in the S&P 500, Apple has almost twenty times more weight than it would have in an index in which stocks are weighted equally. One can justify this overweighting of Apple because a 10% price move by Apple will create more wealth than a 10% price move by the smallest firm in the S&P 500. If the S&P 500 increases 2% in a day, it would be reasonable to think that the market had created 2% more wealth for those who invested in S&P 500 stocks.

The S&P 500 gives you a target you can use to judge your portfolio performance. Of course, if you are primarily trading in stocks that are not part of the S&P 500, then you still do not know what is happening in the part of the market in which you are trading.

3. OTHER MEASURES OF THE MARKET

There are many other indexes that are published daily that measure what is happening in the stock market. Most indexes are capitalization-weighted and are calculated in a fashion similar to the S&P 500. I will mention three more S&P indexes: the S&P MidCap 400, the S&P SmallCap 600, and the S&P Composite 1500. An investor does not need a PhD to ascertain that the S&P MidCap 400 has 400 stocks of medium-size companies (i.e., the largest companies that are not in the S&P 500). The S&P SmallCap 600 has 600 companies that are smaller than the ones in the S&P 400 MidCap. The S&P 1500 is simply all three S&P indexes combined.

Although stock indexes tend to move together, they do not move in lockstep; otherwise, investors would not need all of these variations of indexes. It is important to pick the index that comes closest to matching the stocks that are in your portfolio.

This will give you the best idea about whether or not the portfolio is matching the market's performance.

Russell Investments also publishes several indexes, including the Russell 3000 and the Russell 2500. The Russell 3000 Index measures the performance of the largest 3,000 companies in the US, representing approximately 98% of all investable securities. It is a market capitalization index and is calculated in a fashion similar to the S&P 500. The Russell 2500 Index represents the smallest 2,500 capitalization stocks in the Russell 3000.

The list of variations of indexes and averages is extensive, and I will not attempt to cover them all. It is important for investors to find an index that matches the style of stocks in their portfolio. This will allow investors to evaluate if they are matching what the market is doing. Indexes will become very important later in this book because one of my primary recommendations is that you buy an index mutual fund that simply tries to match the returns from one of the indexes. It will be important for you to understand what assortment of stocks are in the index mutual fund that you are buying so that you understand the amount of risk you are assuming.

WHAT IS THE MARKET DOING?

We now have several options for answering the question, how is the market doing? This may sound like much ado about nothing; it is, however, a very important measure, because professional money managers are trying to beat "the market." Market return is the target everyone is trying to beat, and the ability to beat the market will be used to judge the success and failure of money managers. Since many investors are paying professional investment advisors to beat the market, how one defines the market is very important. These indexes do not move in lockstep; consequently, which index an investor chooses as the target could have a profound effect on what is considered a successful year.

In the fifty-two weeks prior to June 2015, the S&P 500 increased 7.89%, while the stocks on the NASDAQ (the second-largest stock exchange in the world that tends to trade smaller companies than the NYSE) increased 17.02%. Is a 10% return over that same period good or bad? The answer depends on where an investor has his or her money invested. If an investor had his or her money invested in S&P 500 stocks, the investor had a successful year. But if the money was invested in NASDAQ stocks, then the year was not good. The relevant answer to the question of how the stock market is doing for an investor depends on the stocks in the investor's portfolio. If one's portfolio contains primarily large companies, then the S&P 500 is a good target. If one's portfolio is comprised mainly of small companies, however, then the NASDAQ index might be a more suitable target.

So how is the market doing? It depends on what you mean by "the market."

**I don't know if I am a winner or a loser.
Half of the indexes say I am a winner and half say I am a loser.**

MUTUAL FUNDS

Investing in the mutual fund industry is how most individuals (including me) participate in the stock market. A mutual fund is simply a type of professionally managed investment fund that pools the money of many investors who have similar interests and wish to purchase the same type of stocks. One way to view the mutual fund industry is to divide the industry into two categories: *actively* managed mutual funds and *passively* managed mutual funds. Actively managed funds hire a portfolio manager who tries to find undervalued stocks, so the investor in the mutual fund will earn above-market returns (remember, defining market returns can be problematic). These portfolio managers, of course, have to charge fees in order to pay for their time, expertise, and the staff members who help look for undervalued stocks. Consequently, they not only have to beat the market but also have to beat the market by *more* than the fees they are charging. Otherwise, the investor will earn less than market return. As indicated in the Introduction, the empirical evidence indicates that this is an impossible task. If all stocks in the market were traded by mutual fund companies, the mutual fund industry would have to work in Lake Wobegon, where everyone is above average. In the mythical Lake Wobegon, all mutual fund investors could earn an average return after they paid their fees because all mutual funds could earn above-average returns. If having all mutual funds earning above-average market returns sounds impossible, it is. It should not surprise anyone at this point that one of the recommendations of this book will be to *avoid* actively managed mutual funds. After fees, it is almost impossible for most actively managed mutual funds to beat the stock market average, Lake Wobegon notwithstanding.

Passively managed index mutual funds do not try to beat the market; they simply try to *match* one of the indexes. An index mutual fund will pick the index that it plans to try to match and then buy all the stocks in that index, thereby allowing it to match the returns of that index. The advantage that index funds have over actively managed funds is that they do not have to hire portfolio managers and staff to try to find undervalued stocks; index funds just passively buy stocks in the index. This advantage allows them to have costs significantly lower than those of an actively managed mutual fund. This cost advantage is passed along to the mutual fund shareholder. Over long periods of time, this cost advantage can mean tens of thousands of dollars to the account holder.

Another advantage a passively managed mutual fund has over an actively managed mutual fund is federal income tax savings. A capital gains tax liability is created when a stock is sold for more than the purchase price of that stock. Even if you have a significant paper gain, you do not owe capital gains tax *until that stock is sold*. For mutual funds, these tax liabilities are passed on to the mutual fund shareholder. Since index funds have very little turnover in their portfolio, they create very little capital gains tax liability for their shareholders. Actively managed funds, on the other hand, can have a very high turnover rate in their portfolio, thus creating capital gains tax liabilities for the shareholder. If you reinvest all dividends and capital gains, you have a tax obligation—without any cash from the mutual fund to pay for the tax. With an index mutual fund, however, most of your capital gains will occur when you sell the mutual fund—and can then use the proceeds from that sale to pay your taxes.

BEST VS. SUITABLE

Although one of the primary purposes of this book is to teach you what you need to know to make your own investment decisions, if you find yourself in a position where you think you need external advice, it is important to know what types of investment advisors are available to you—and to understand their differences. These differences were briefly mentioned earlier in the book; they are substantial, however, and it is important to examine them more closely.

Advisors who have a fiduciary responsibility to their clients are typically referred to simply as "fiduciaries." As stated previously, fiduciaries must, by law, remove any potential conflicts of interest and put the needs of clients above their own. If you engage a fiduciary, you will pay a fee (usually an hourly rate or a percentage of your assets). What you pay the fiduciary is the same whether you follow the advice or choose to ignore it. Although not all fiduciaries are created equal (i.e., some will provide better advice than others), at least you know that the fiduciary is giving you the best advice he or she has available. Due diligence is essential, and it is the investor's responsibility to find a fiduciary who has a stellar reputation. Search the information available on the Internet and ask friends and colleagues about advisors they have used. Ask fiduciaries what professional organizations(s) they belong to and how long they have been in business, then request a list of clients you can contact for references. It is important to do your homework before investing your hard-earned money.

Although brokers may provide good advice and may have excellent products to sell, in general they make their money by selling particular products. By law, a broker is only required to sell a "suitable" (a legal term) product, and unlike fiduciaries, brokers are not required to remove all potential conflicts of interest, nor are they required to put the needs of clients above their own. Ask yourself whose interest is being served if you purchase an investment product from a person who earns a commission on the sale of the product. Investors should demand the products that are best suited to their needs, not just "suitable" products.

In the movie *Liar, Liar*, the main character (played by Jim Carrey) is unable to lie. After a sexual encounter, he tells his lover, "I've had better." As you might imagine, this does not go over well with the lover. When you receive investment advice, you do not want to end up saying, "It could have been better." Does anyone want to have dinner in a "suitable" restaurant or take a "suitable" vacation when the *best* is available at the same price? Why then would you want to purchase "suitable" investment products?

Investors should require—and demand—the best available investment advice and products for their needs.

SUMMARY

You should now be familiar with some of the more important concepts every investor should know. You understand that there are a variety of measures of market performance, each tailored to different kinds of stock holdings, and that the old favorite, the Dow, is the least representative of the stock market. You should, of course, use the indicator of market performance that best reflects your own stock holdings; this will allow you to make an intelligent determination about the performance of your portfolio.

You also understand that there are two kinds of mutual funds—actively managed and passively managed—and that passively managed mutual funds are almost always the best choice. In addition, you know to use a fiduciary if you need any investment advice.

As you invest in the market, you will run across other important concepts that are not covered in this chapter, but for now, you should have a good grasp of the basic concepts and vocabulary to allow you to start your investment program.

CHAPTER 3

SOCIAL SECURITY

When I began writing this book, I thought I would have at most a few paragraphs dealing with Social Security. I never imagined I would devote an entire chapter to the topic! I teach public finance, a senior-level undergraduate course taken by many senior economics majors. The course briefly covers Social Security. As part of my preparation for writing this book, I reviewed what I already knew about the Social Security system and then went into more depth on some of the finer points of the system. Social Security is complicated; there are over 2,000 rules and thousands of pages explaining how these rules should be applied.[16]

In this chapter, I am not going to try to explain even a small fraction of the subtleties of Social Security, but I hope to give you a high-level overview of some of the more commonly used features of Social Security. If you want a much fuller account, I again recommend the book *Get What's Yours* by Kotlikoff, Moeller, and Solman.

Because of current problems with the Social Security system, it is highly likely that the 2,000 rules will be modified in the near future. Given this prediction, you might ask why you should even read this chapter if you are younger than sixty. Although it is fairly clear that Social Security needs reform, it is not clear what form the modifications will take. For the past thirty years, I have been telling my students to assume that Social Security will not be there when they retire. I have personally done my own retirement planning with the same assumption. However, although Social Security has changed significantly over the past thirty years (e.g., a change in the age of full retirement, cost-of-living adjustments, etc.), the system has remained quite resilient. Even with the current uncertainty surrounding Social Security, it is probably a good idea for everyone to have some understanding of how Social Security works today, even if major changes do take place in the future. Also, even if you are not near retirement age, you may know someone who is approaching that passage and could use your help with their Social Security planning.

IT REALLY IS A BIG NEST EGG

In 2014, the US Social Security Administration reported that the maximum monthly Social Security retirement payment for workers claiming benefits at full retirement age (FRA) was $2,639.[17] Most individuals will have a monthly income from Social Security less than $2,639, and some who wait until age seventy to begin receiving benefits will have an income greater than this figure.[18] Although designed to be a *supplement* (this is an important point), Social Security has become the major source of retirement income for millions of Americans. Even for families whose incomes are in the top quintile of income, Social Security benefits represent (on average) 29% of annual household income. In households whose head is currently between sixty-five and sixty-nine years of age, the current median expected value of lifetime benefits is $230,000 for singles and $470,000 for couples.[19] For high-income families (90th percentile), the expected value of benefits is in excess of $500,000.[20] The takeaway is that Social Security can represent a significant part of a family's wealth and income in retirement.

The decision you make regarding *when* to start collecting Social Security benefits is probably the most important decision you will make with regard to Social Security. This choice can have a dramatic impact on how much Social Security you will collect over your lifetime. The next section will help you understand what you need to consider as you plan when to start collecting benefits. It is important to emphasize that when you retire from employment and when you start drawing Social Security benefits does not necessarily have to be the same and can, in fact, differ by many years. For example, you could start collecting Social Security at sixty-two and continue to work full-time (almost always a mistake), or you could retire at sixty-six and delay collecting Social Security until age seventy (which can be a good strategy).

WHEN TO COLLECT BENEFITS

Those who qualify to receive regular Social Security benefits can start collecting benefits at any age from sixty-two to seventy. The longer you wait, the higher the monthly benefit. The following chart illustrates this point.

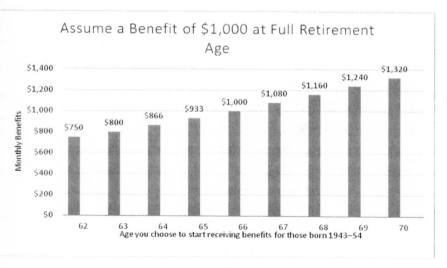

Source: ssa.gov

If you were born between 1943–54, the current full retirement age, or FRA, is sixty-six (that will increase over time to sixty-seven). For persons born between 1943–54, if your Social Security benefits are $1,000 a month at full retirement age and you started drawing Social Security at age sixty-two, you would receive $750 a month—a 25% reduction from your FRA benefits. On the other hand, if you delayed your collection of Social Security benefits until age seventy, you would receive $1,320 per month—8% more for each year after your FRA (or 76% more per month) than if you started collecting at age sixty-two. There is no reason to start collecting Social Security benefits later than your seventieth birthday; the monthly benefits do not increase after that date.

Of course, for each month you wait to collect Social Security, you will receive one less month of benefits. The question then becomes, when is the optimum time to start collecting Social Security benefits? It should not surprise you that the answer depends on several variables.

I would like to emphasize once again that when you stop working and when you start collecting Social Security do *not* have to be the same. Although you can still work full-time and collect Social Security *before* your FRA, in most cases there is a *substantial reduction* in your monthly Social Security benefits. Once you reach your FRA, you can continue to work and, without penalty, collect the full amount of Social Security you are entitled to receive. Under the current Social Security rules, there is a strong incentive *not* to claim benefits until you have either retired or reached your FRA.

In 2012, 43% of women and 38% of men in the US started collecting Social Security benefits at age sixty-two. Only 1% of men and 2% of women waited until age seventy to start collecting their Social Security benefits; another 2% of men and 2% of women started collecting between the ages of sixty-seven and sixty-nine. This means that over 96% of the population who are eligible for Social Security benefits took their retirement benefits at FRA or before.[21] The question you should ask at this point is whether individuals are making the correct choices regarding when to start collecting Social Security benefits.

One way to approach this question is to do a breakeven analysis; I will explain later, however, why this may not be the optimum approach. A breakeven analysis requires you to compare A (the total amount you would receive if you drew a higher monthly payment for a shorter time period) to B (the total amount you would receive if you drew a lower monthly payment for a longer time period). You would then determine how many months it would take for the totals of these two payment options to be equal.

Using the chart above, assume you are considering retiring at age sixty-two, when your Social Security check would be $750; the other option you are considering is retiring at age sixty-six (your FRA), when your monthly Social Security would be $1,000. If you retired and started benefits at sixty-two, you would collect the $750 per month benefit for four years (forty-eight months) longer than you would collect the $1,000 per month benefit you would receive if you retired and started benefits at age sixty-six. The breakeven number of months can be calculated as follows (don't you just love algebra?):

$$750 (X + 48) = 1,000 X$$

X is the number of months it takes to break even. In this particular case, X = 144 or twelve years.

The result is that at age seventy-eight (your FRA plus the twelve years, i.e., 66 + 12), you would have collected the same amount of money from Social Security whether you started at age sixty-two or age sixty-six. If you lived beyond age seventy-eight and waited until age sixty-six to begin benefits, you would end up collecting more from Social Security than if you chose to start collecting at sixty-two.

Most of us are not able to predict when we will die; if you anticipate, however, that you will most likely live longer than the number of months you calculate in a breakeven analysis (in this example, 144 months), you should defer collecting Social Security. If, however, you have reason to think you are likely to live a shorter amount of time than the number of months you calculated in the breakeven analysis, you should begin collecting Social Security benefits immediately.

The Social Security Administration has calculated Social Security benefits on an actuarial fair basis:[22] hence, the person with an average lifespan will receive the same total Social Security payments regardless of when Social Security benefits are started. This means that the Social Security Administration pays out the same aggregate benefits regardless of when retirees decide to start Social Security benefits.

The Social Security office used to do a breakeven calculation for individuals, but they no longer do, in part because they concluded it was a misleading way to think about when to start Social Security. Most financial planners also think that a breakeven analysis is not the correct way to decide when to start Social Security benefits,[23] and I agree with them.

Instead of thinking about the breakeven point for Social Security, you should think about the substantial risks you could face during retirement. Social Security not only reduces these risks but also reduces them more if you wait longer to collect it. Waiting longer to claim Social Security benefits can help reduce three very important risks individuals face in retirement:

- longevity risk,
- inflation risk, and
- market risk.

The first kind of risk Social Security helps ameliorate is *longevity risk*: the risk that you will outlive your retirement savings. Very few people feel confident that they have enough savings to last them throughout their lifetime.[24] As Kotlikoff, Moeller, and Solman point out in their book *Get What's Yours*, "Life's biggest danger isn't dying, it's living."[25] One way to reduce this concern is to wait as long as possible to start collecting Social Security benefits. By waiting to start collecting Social Security, you will have increased your monthly payments from Social Security, thus requiring you to use less of your retirement savings each month after you retire. Of course, you will have to use more of these savings if you retire well before you start collecting Social Security, but almost all financial experts agree that in most cases, waiting is a wise strategy.

**100th birthday! I can afford this because
I delayed collecting Social Security.**

The second risk Social Security helps ameliorate is *inflation risk*: the risk your money will not buy the same level of goods and services in the future that it buys today. Over time, inflation can severely erode your purchasing power—especially during retirement, when you are not working and receiving raises. Social Security currently has an annual cost-of-living adjustment. This cost-of-living hedge means that if your other sources of income are not indexed to inflation, at least you have a partial buffer against the erosion of your purchasing power during retirement. Because of this cost-of-living adjustment, the purchasing power of the monthly Social Security benefits you start with should remain approximately the same over the remainder of your life. The greater the percentage of your retirement income that comes from Social Security, the less you will have to worry about the erosion of your purchasing power in retirement. While other sources of retirement income may not keep up with inflation, Social Security should. This is a tremendous benefit of the current Social Security system, and the larger your base Social Security payment is, the larger your cost-of-living adjustment will be. Of course, like all provisions of Social Security, this cost-of-living provision is subject to change.

The third kind of risk Social Security helps reduce is *market risk*: the risk that you will have to draw down your assets at the worse possible moment (i.e., sell stocks at a low price). This risk is especially troublesome for retirees who must draw down assets to help cover their monthly expenses. Unfortunately, that is most retirees. Asset drawdowns are especially painful when the stock market is in a prolonged bear market. The years 2007–08 are a clear example of how a down market can have devastating effects on one's portfolio. If you wait to collect benefits, however, you will not have to sell as many assets in a down market, because your monthly Social Security payments will be higher.

Even with its major flaws—and it *does* have major flaws— Social Security plays an important role in the lives of most US citizens. Virtually everyone who earns a paycheck pays Social Security tax, and almost everyone of retirement age receives some form of Social Security benefits. Any politician who would attempt to drastically reduce Social Security benefits would surely risk political suicide. The three features of Social Security listed above would be hard to duplicate in the private market.

AND THE ANSWER IS …

The short answer regarding *when* to start Social Security benefits is to wait as long as you can. This means that when you retire, you pay your living expenses out of savings and if possible, defer collecting Social Security until age seventy. This conclusion is supported by academic research, as well as advice from most financial planners.[26] If you follow this advice, you will receive more income per month but will collect for fewer months. Appreciate and concentrate on the longevity factor, the inflation safety net, and the market protection that Social Security provides.

Although waiting to begin collecting your Social Security benefits until age seventy (when you would receive the maximum monthly payment) is optimal, there are, of course, exceptions to this rule. If you are age sixty-two or older and need the money to pay current expenses, then you will need to start benefits sooner. If you have never been married and have a short life expectancy, then sooner rather than later will make sense. Notice I stated "if you have never been married and have a short life expectancy." You might think that if you have a short life expectancy, you should *always* file sooner rather than later. The complicating factor, however, is that a spouse and/or ex-spouse(s) has a right to a survivor benefit based on your Social Security record, and this benefit continues to increase until you reach your FRA. There may be times when you want to delay your benefit even though you have a short life expectancy, so that your "survivors" can receive larger Social Security payments. There are many factors that go into the calculation of survivor benefits. If you are in such a situation, you will need to do your homework or get advice from someone who is very familiar with the policies and regulations governing Social Security survivor benefits.

In summary, in most cases it is better to use the assets at your disposal to pay for living expenses during the first years of retirement and defer receiving Social Security benefits until your seventieth birthday. It has been estimated that an average couple's expected lifetime benefit will increase if both individuals wait until they are age seventy to begin collecting Social Security.[27]

It is important to remember the three risks factors that Social Security helps ameliorate: longevity risk, inflation risk, and market risk.

WHAT YOU SEE TODAY MAY NOT BE WHAT YOU GET TOMORROW

"One of the little-known quirks of the current Social Security system is something the Social Security system calls 'file and suspend ...' " Thus began a long section of my first draft of this book in which I explained how certain individuals could "file and suspend" Social Security benefits and earn up to $50,000 of extra benefits. As of May 1, 2016, this provision has been removed from the Social Security system; hence, several pages of my first draft have been deleted. I mention this only to illustrate that what you see today in Social Security may not be there tomorrow.

ADDITIONAL BENEFITS

In addition to the retirement benefits and spousal benefits that Social Security provides, there are also:

- Spousal benefits for those caring for an eligible child or children
- Child benefits for young children of retirees
- Child benefits for disabled children of retirees, regardless of the child's age
- Divorced spousal benefits
- Widow/widower survivor benefits

As you can see, the Social Security system is very complicated and tries to do many things for many people. This is, of course, a strength, but it is also one of the primary reasons the system is running out of funds. The original purpose of instituting a system where you paid Social Security taxes and then received those monies back with interest has long ago been abandoned.

Be warned: It is not easy to figure out if you are receiving everything you are entitled to receive from the Social Security system, and finding good advice is not always easy, either. In the end, you will need to deal with the individuals who work for the Social Security Administration. My personal experience has been that these people do a good job of overseeing a very complicated system. Unless you are trying to do something that is easy and straightforward, however, in order to make sure you are receiving the highest benefits the law allows, you need to do your own research *before* you go to the Social Security office. The agency gets more than three million requests for information every week.[28] You need to remember that the Social Security representative is providing you *information*, not advice about what you should do. It is important to do your own research.

FUTURE OF SOCIAL SECURITY

When Harry Truman was in the White House, economists would come to the president's office to brief him on the status of the US and world economies. The economists would often say, "On the one hand . . . but on the other hand . . ."[29] This became very frustrating for President Truman, who ordered his chief of staff to allow only "one-handed" economists to visit the president. It is usually very difficult to get an economist to give a definite answer to any question. President Truman was looking for an economist who was not trying to cover all the bases.

I will now pretend to be a one-handed economist: The Social Security system will change in the near future. (Okay, so I really did not stick my neck out very much.) The way the current system is constructed is not sustainable into the future. Some individuals believe that both the money they have paid into Social Security plus the interest earned is sitting there waiting for them when they retire. The reality is that soon after the Social Security Act was passed in 1935, it was transformed from a traditional pension plan to a pay-as-you-go system. Practically speaking, this means there is a transfer of money from those who are currently working to those who collect Social Security—from current workers to retired workers. The only way to receive Social Security benefits is to convince those who are currently working to continue to pay their Social Security taxes. When we cover Social Security in class, I tell my students the only reason I am nice to them is that I want them to pay their Social Security tax, so when I retire I can receive the Social Security benefits I so richly deserve.

The funding problems of Social Security were seen from the very beginning. The Social Security Act was enacted in 1935, and by 1937–38, an advisory council had been appointed to make reform recommendations.[30] One of the issues that was discussed was changing the Social Security system from a pension-plan model to a pay-as-you-go system. An important reason for the switch was the fact that the savings of many of the elderly had been wiped out by the Great Depression, and it was widely thought the elderly deserved to be supported by more than the small sum they had contributed to Social Security. The advisory council discussed the fact that if they changed the Social Security system to a pay-as-you-go system, they would create tremendous cost obligations for future generations. But they changed the model anyway. It is nice to know that kicking the can down the road is not a new phenomenon.

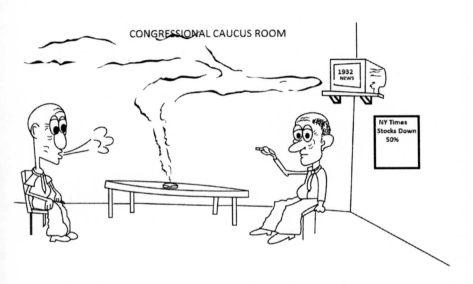

By the time these Social Security problems become acute, we will be dead.

The Social Security shortfall has become acute, and it is getting close to the time when some hard choices must be made. The trustees of Social Security project that the annual deficit will average about $69 billion between 2016 and 2019.[31]

On April 15, 2015, the *Wall Street Journal* reported that Governor Chris Christie—who, at the time, was contemplating running for president—was calling to scale back Social Security benefits for some Americans. Christie suggested he would shift Social Security from its New Deal origins as a retirement vehicle for nearly all working Americans to a program that taxes all workers but does not pay benefits to those with the highest incomes. We now know how this suggestion worked out for Governor Christie.

All proposed fixes must boil down to some combination of these three options: raise taxes, lower benefits, and/or take money from another tax source. The can has been kicked to the end of the road.

DISABILITY UNDER SOCIAL SECURITY

Part of the strength of Social Security—but also one of its weaknesses—is that it has become a greater percentage of retirement income for retirees than was ever intended when it was first proposed.

Just as Social Security has become the dominant source of income for most older Americans, so has it become the nation's default welfare program. Neither role was part of the agency's founding mission, which envisioned Social Security as a modest source of supplement income to augment people's savings and pensions. Yet here the program finds itself, some 80 years later, paying out benefits under two programs to more than 20 million disabled Americans. That's a huge number in its own right and even more so considering how many additional lives and livelihoods are affected by the 200 billion in annual benefits the disabled receive. (Kotlikoff, Moeller, and Solman, *Get What's Yours*, p. 187)

Supplemental Security Income (SSI) is for disabled adults and disabled children with limited income and resources. Social Security Disability Insurance (SSDI) is available to workers who have been determined to be disabled and have worked and paid Social Security payroll taxes for the requisite number of quarters according to Social Security guidelines. The rules for qualifying for either SSI or SSDI programs are beyond the scope of this book. But you should be aware that when it comes to qualifying for either program, barely one-third of disability applicants are determined eligible for the programs when they initially apply. Many of those who are denied hire lawyers to appeal their denials, with a national average of 13% winning their appeals.[32] If you think you might qualify for either program, it is important to do your homework before applying.

Finally, you should know that the SSDI program is scheduled to run short of money in 2016.

SUMMARY

For many years, the majority of retired US citizens have depended on Social Security as the backbone of their retirement income. It has been especially helpful for the least wealthy and has significantly lowered poverty rates for older Americans.[33] Unfortunately, the current construction of the system is not sustainable. If you are close to retirement, you can still benefit from the program but would be wise to delay receiving Social Security payments for as long as possible. If you are not near retirement, you should already have begun the serious business of building your own investment portfolio. That's why you're reading this book!

CHAPTER 4

THE STOCK MARKET

BUY LOW, SELL HIGH

I have found the perfect way to begin my undergraduate investment course. At the start of the first class, I walk into the classroom and announce that there are only two rules for investing. I turn to the board and write "Rule 1: *Buy Low, Sell High*." I turn back to the class and ask if there are any questions regarding Rule 1. At that point, a nervous quiet usually permeates the room. I am sure some students are thinking, *I paid more than $50,000 a year to the university to take a course that has no more substance than this?*

With no questions, I turn to the board again and write "Rule 2: *Don't Forget Rule 1*." I again ask if there are any questions. In the thirty years I have taught the course, I have never had a student ask a question after I write down the two rules.

I then announce the date, time, and location of the final exam, pick up my books and notes, head to the door, and leave the room for a few seconds. Then, of course, I return and say that perhaps there are a few details we should discuss before the end of the semester ...

We then spend the semester trying to master some of the complicated investment theories that have been constructed by academics over the past seventy years. These investment theories can drive even university professors to distraction. Economists have received Nobel Prizes for enhancing what we understand about the investment world. Students often tell me that the investment course is one of the most difficult they take during their undergraduate career. Unfortunately for the students enrolled in my investment class, the final exam indeed covers more than the two rules for investing that I write on the board the first day of class.

Are you sure there is not more to investing than that?

Although it is hard to believe, one of the biggest mistakes stock investors make is the violation of Rule 1. A review of stock market history reveals that investors do not buy low and sell high and that, in fact, many investors buy high and sell low. This seems astonishing, but in general, human beings are more comfortable moving *with* the crowd than against it. John Maynard Keynes, who has been called the father of modern macroeconomics, once wrote, "Worldly wisdom teaches that it is better for reputations to fail conventionally than to succeed unconventionally."[34]

Rule 1 requires an individual to buy stocks when the stock market is declining and the financial news is at its worse; when everyone else seems to be selling, driving down the price of stocks, individuals actually need to be buying. Those who buy low must purchase stocks when the conventional wisdom is to sell. In other words, you must be a contrarian. And if you are a true contrarian, you will be happy when the market is down 10% and view this as an opportunity to buy stocks; if the stock market continues down and drops by 20%, you will buy more stocks and be even happier.

From October 9, 2007 to March 9, 2009, the average US company lost more than 50% of its total stock market value.[35] This was a real test for those of us who preach buying low and selling high. During 2008, people who knew what I did for a living would often stop me and tell me how worried and frightened they thought I must be because the market was going down. Instead, I responded positively—the down market was allowing me to follow the first part of Rule 1: Buy low. I would, of course, have been singing a different tune if my circumstances had made it necessary for me to sell stocks during that period. Fortunately for me, I was in the accumulation phase of life and saw it as a great opportunity to buy. I was confident the US economy would prosper in the future, and the stock market would return to its historic highs.

As the history of individual investment in the stock market would have predicted, in the most recent significant bear market of 2007–09, many investors "rode the bear" (i.e., held their stocks) to near the bottom of the market. As the market neared the bottom, when investors feared they would lose everything, they sold much, if not all, of their stock portfolio at very low prices. In other words, they sold low. In 2015, when the markets again reached record highs, many investors were trying to get back into the market, and they were buying high.

Human nature leads individuals to want to be on the bandwagon when the stock market is rising, but when the market is falling, everyone wants off the wagon. Some economists estimate that typical investors lose as much as 5.3% per year from violating Rule 1.[36] Most estimates of investors' losses resulting from buying high and selling low are in the 1.5% to 2% per year range. The successful investor will have a contrarian streak and will not, as Keynes warned, be afraid to succeed unconventionally.

An investor can potentially earn an additional 2% or more per year over the average investor who does not follow Rule 1. What can this extra 2% per year mean to a young investor? If a young investor puts aside $100 per month for forty years (a total investment of $48,000), the difference between earning 8% versus 10% per year is an extra $250,000. Moral to the story: Remember Rule 1.

The above illustrates the focus of this book: simple rules that will allow you to earn a higher average return than that earned by most investment professionals. If you follow Rule 1, you will not be one of the typical investors who euphorically buys and then, when panicked, sells. You will be an investor who has a plan in place and will not deviate from the plan when the winds of despair hit Wall Street. Any investor who runs with the investment crowd is doomed to lose several percent per year compared to average stock market return.

HOW TO OUTPERFORM THE PROS

The above section illustrates one of the reasons why the typical investor does not earn even the average return from the stock market. Over long periods, the stock market has yielded approximately 10% per year. On the other hand, the average investor has earned approximately 7% per year. One of the purposes of this book is to help you eliminate most of this 3% loss. This loss occurs mainly because of bad timing (buying high and selling low) and hiring professional money managers (their boat payment) in a futile effort to try to beat the market average. I will show you how you can easily avoid this 3% drag on your investment portfolio. This is how you are going to earn a higher return than the average investor. As a bonus, I will also show you how you can tilt a portfolio so you might even earn higher-than-market returns.

One of the most important elements of successful investing is concentrating on the variables that can be controlled and not worrying about the variables that cannot be controlled. As you can imagine, when it comes to investing, there are very few variables an individual can control. Those you can control, however, are extremely important and can have a dramatic impact on the return you will earn from your investments.

You cannot control interest rates, unemployment, inflation, oil prices, etc., so there is no need to factor these variables into your thinking when constructing your portfolio. The current price of a stock will already reflect all the relevant information—both good and bad—that is available to the public; this is the essence of an efficient market.

There are two elements you *can* control, however: costs and the allocation of monies among various investment options. Control these two elements intelligently, and you can have hundreds of thousands of extra dollars in your investment account.

As a caveat, I cannot tell anyone how to get rich quick (exceptions: pick the correct parents, marry into money, or start your own business, become wildly successful, and sell to Google), and neither can anyone else. If an individual who can consistently beat the stock market average exists, it would take more than ten years to differentiate that skilled person from those who are simply lucky. To illustrate this point, consider the group of professional portfolio money managers who must make their record available to the public (i.e., the mutual fund industry). There are approximately 3,000 mutual funds in the US. Assume that half of these professional money managers will beat the market in any one year because of good luck (a reasonable assumption) and that the other half will lose to the average because of bad luck. At the end of eight years, approximately twelve money managers will have beaten the average eight years in a row—just because of good luck.

Year	Number of winners who continue to win (assuming 50/50 chance of winning)
Start	3,000
1	1,500
2	750
3	375
4	188
5	94
6	47
7	24
8	12

As my father used to say, "I would rather be lucky than good." We know that these twelve winners beat the average not by their skill in choosing stocks but because the game is constructed so that half the players are winners because of luck—and half are losers. Does anyone want to jump on the bandwagon of these twelve winners, knowing they have only beaten the market because of good luck?

This illustrates the challenge when choosing a mutual fund that has had a great historical record over the past eight or more years. Is this money manager exceptional or just lucky?

The odds are very high that the portfolio manager who beat the average is just lucky. The challenge for an investor is to distinguish the truly great investment guru from the ones who are just lucky. The lucky ones will all have great stories to explain their success. I have never heard an investment manager state, "I was just lucky to have beaten the market average." By the time you find the individual or individuals who are brilliant instead of just lucky, however, it is probably too late to invest in their fund—either because they have retired or because the fund is so large they cannot duplicate what they have done in the past with smaller amounts of money.

Of course, Warren Buffett is a brilliant money manager. He has written a remarkable record over several decades and has become one of the richest persons in the world. Warren is not lucky; he is really good. Your task is to find the new young Warren Buffett. Where is he or she? I wish I knew.

In my investment class, I do the following exercise. I have all the students stand up and take out a coin, then flip it in the air. Heads are winners, and tails are losers, and only the winner can continue playing the game; the losers have to sit down. The winners repeat the flip, with heads being winners, and tails being losers. We continue the game until someone has flipped six or seven heads in a row. I walk up to that person and tell them that they are the greatest coin flipper of all time—and that I am going to invest with them. Of course, in the next few flips, they get tails. Then I tell them to sit down and that I am very disappointed.

The lesson here is that in the short run, many money managers can beat the market because of luck, but over time, the averages tend to fall back to the market average. In fact, there are studies that show that the best strategy to follow when choosing an actively managed mutual fund is to select one that is in the bottom quartile in terms of performance. These funds are much more likely to outperform the market than one in the top quartile.[37] The top quartile funds tend to fall back to the market average, and the bottom quartile tend to rise up to the market average. This is what is commonly referred to as *regression to the mean*. This fact demonstrates how hard it is to separate the gifted money managers from the lucky ones.

Your guess is as good as mine is. That will be $500.

At one point in time, hedge funds (a pooled investment vehicle) were the darlings of Wall Street. Many investment advisors thought this was the wise way to invest. A *New York Times* article from May 5, 2015, however, stated that 2014 was the sixth consecutive year in which hedge funds had fallen short of stock market performance, returning only 3% (on average) over that six-year period.[38] In 2014, the average return for hedge funds was in the low single digits, while the S&P 500 stocks index posted a gain of 13.68% when dividends were reinvested.

Investors in hedge funds generally pay an annual management fee of 2% of the assets under management and 20% of any profits. The *New York Times* estimated that in 2014, Kenneth C. Griffin, the founder and CEO of Citadel, a hedge fund, took home $1.3 billion. It is hard to believe anyone is worth that much, especially when you do not do as well as the market.

Why can't I afford to fly to Cayman? I own shares in his hedge fund.

Remember: Bulls win, bears win, and pigs lose. Do not chase the latest fad. Slow and steady will win the race.

WHAT DO ECONOMISTS MEAN BY "EFFICIENT MARKETS?"

A standard economist joke begins with an economist and a non-economist walking down the street together. The non-economist says, "Look! There's a $20 bill on the sidewalk." The economist replies by saying, "That's impossible, because if it were really a $20 bill, it would have been picked up by now."

The joke illustrates how economists think about efficient markets. One can also apply this concept of efficiency to

Wal-Mart checkout lanes. Which line is the quickest line? For an economist, the simple answer is that it is not worth searching for the shortest line; if there were a shorter line, people would have already joined it, and it would no longer be the quickest. Extending this logic to the stock market, if the market price of a stock were lower than the "true" value, investors would start buying the stock, driving the price up; instantaneously, the market value would equal the "true" value.

In efficient markets, the $20 bill has already been picked up, there is no need to search for the shortest line, and all stocks are priced at their "true" value.

To further illustrate what an efficient stock market implies, suppose your cousin Tessa tells you to buy a company's stock because it is undervalued, and when the stock returns to its true value, you will earn above-market return. The first thing you should ask Tessa is why all the other brilliant investors have not bought the stock and driven the price up. What does the seller who is willing to sell you the stock know that Tessa does not? It is important to remember that when an investor tries to outsmart the market by buying undervalued stocks, that investor is competing with the collective knowledge of all other investors. There are thousands of very smart investors who are working full-time trying to find undervalued stocks and have millions of dollars at their disposal. Why are they not buying the undervalued company recommended by Tessa?

The philosopher and economist Adam Smith's "invisible hand" (i.e., the idea that persons pursuing their own self-interest will drive the price of stocks to their "true" value) is going to make certain that all stocks are trading at their fair, or intrinsic, value. If the stock market is an efficient market, then without doing any homework, an investor can buy any stock with the assurance that it is fairly priced at any given point in time. The implication is that an investor can rely on the collective wisdom of all investors to keep stock prices at their "fair" price.

The stock market is an efficient market because portfolio managers who evaluate stocks are smart and work very hard. For one portfolio manger to consistently outperform the others, he or she must be smarter and work harder than the others. The manager who consistently outperforms the others would have to constantly find undervalued stocks before the other managers. The empirical evidence is that no portfolio manager can do this over the long run (i.e., the stock market is efficient).

To fully understand what these portfolio managers are doing, an investor would practically need PhDs in mathematics, economics, *and* psychology. If you and your cousin Tessa want to pick stocks that outperform the market, you will need to be better than the professional stock analysts at finding undervalued stocks. The stock market is not Lake Wobegon (that fictional, above-average town). If a group of investors is going to be better than average, another group must be worse than average; this is true not only for professional money managers but also for individual investors who are selecting their own stocks. From this perspective, the stock market becomes what economists call a "zero-sum game": for every winner, there must be a loser. The return earned by both the typical investor and professional money manager must be the average market return, minus any expenses incurred in construction of a portfolio. And since no professional portfolio manager can consistently beat the stock market by picking stocks, the odds that you and Tessa can do it are slim.

You and Tessa, however, can beat the professional net of fees by keeping expenses lower than the expenses of the professionals. This result is due to the stock market being efficient.

The good news is that with the knowledge gained by reading this book, the reader can not only beat the vast majority of professionals who work on Wall Street but also spend no more than a few hours a year on investments. How? By keeping expenses lower than the Wall Street professionals. If investors keep their expenses lower than the pros on Wall Street, the average net return (return minus expenses) will exceed the average net return earned by professional money managers. It's just that simple. Over long periods of time, these small differences in net return can have a dramatic impact on the value of your portfolio. The magnitude of these impacts will be illustrated later in the book.

I bought the same stocks as you but I used an advisor.

FREE LUNCH?

In my economics classes, I tell my students there is "no free lunch." In order to get something of value, one needs to give up something of value. Even if I buy a student's lunch, that student still has to sit and listen to me talk (and forgo an hour of sleep). The stock market, however, may provide the illusive "free lunch." Market forces keep a stock price at what is perceived to be, at that point in time, its true value. An investor does not have to work at searching for undervalued stocks; the Wall Street whiz kids have made the stock market reflect all information available—both good and bad. In a fully efficient stock market, the odds of an investor finding a stock that is undervalued, thus earning more than market return, are zero. An investor has the same odds of finding an undervalued stock by doing research as by throwing a dart at the newspaper stock page and buying the company hit by the darts. As a result of an efficient stock market, an investor does not have to do the arduous work of looking for undervalued stocks.

Not only does it logically follow that the stock market should be efficient; there is also compelling empirical evidence.[39] Some of the best evidence comes from stock mutual funds. The mutual fund industry is enormous, with $15 trillion in assets under management at year-end 2013.[40] In a *New York Times* article, Jeff Sommer wrote, "The truth is that very few professional investors have actually managed to outperform the rising market consistently; in fact, based on the updated findings, it appears that no mutual fund managers have."[41]

Given that the stock market is efficient, this leads to one of the main pieces of advice contained in this book: If you cannot *beat* the market average, you should at least earn the market average return by buying an index mutual fund. The implication is that instead of trying to buy stocks or buy actively managed mutual funds that will fail to match the market average after they pay their expenses, investors should "join the average." The upshot is that investors should buy index funds that do not try to beat the average but rather *match* the average. These index funds beat the net return of managed mutual funds by keeping expenses low. This low-fee structure allows the funds to come closer to the market average than funds with high expense ratios. This is one of the mantras of this book: Keep expenses low. By buying an index fund, you receive all the benefits of all the active money managers (i.e., you get a free lunch).

The *Wall Street Journal* used to run a contest. They hired a monkey to throw darts at a newspaper page filled with stocks, then had stock analysts also pick stocks. After a period of time, they reviewed how the stock analysts and monkey had done in terms of market returns: Monkey vs. Wall Street—the Game of Markets. Not surprising to efficient market proponents, the monkey won about half the time, and the stock analysts won the other half (which, by the way, are exactly the results you would expect to see if all stocks were properly priced when the contest began).

But I did win ... half of the time.

The *Wall Street Journal* no longer has such a contest. I would guess one of the reasons the contest was discontinued was that it made it very difficult for stock analysts to justify their six-figure salaries if they were beaten by a dart-throwing monkey half the time.

THREE FORMS OF THE EFFICIENT MARKET HYPOTHESIS

While I have stated that I believe the stock market is efficient, there are actually three forms of the efficient market hypothesis:

- weak,
- semi-strong, and
- strong.

These three forms of the efficient market hypothesis are related to how stock analysts attempt to find undervalued stocks. The weak form of the efficient market hypothesis is related to technical analysis, the semi-strong is related to fundamental analysis, and the strong form is the ultimate efficient market hypothesis.

In the next sections, I will provide short descriptions of how technical analysis, fundamental analysis, and the ultimate efficient markets hypothesis are supposed to work—and explain why I think the semi-strong form of the efficient market hypothesis offers the best way to view the stock market.

TECHNICAL ANALYSIS/WEAK FORM OF THE EFFICIENT MARKET HYPOTHESIS

Technical analysts find undervalued stocks by looking at price movement patterns over time and comparing those patterns to historic patterns. Technical analysts are convinced that stocks will follow the same pattern in the future as stocks did in the past. In other words, history *does* repeat itself when it comes to stock price movements. Once they find a historic pattern similar to a current pattern, analysts know how the stock will behave in the future. All they need to do is find a stock that has a price movement that history shows will lead to large gains, buy that stock, and hold it as the price increases. When the pattern has run its course and is no longer in an up-movement phase, they sell the stock.

When I teach investments, we spend very little class time dealing with technical analysis. There is strong evidence that technical analysis does not succeed in finding undervalued stocks.[42] Computers have been programmed to search thousands of stocks over scores of years, and patterns have been found in only a few cases. The patterns that have been found do not allow an investor to earn above-market returns after taxes and the cost of trading.

As I tell my students, for technical analysis to work, you would have to find a pattern no one else has found. Possessing unique knowledge is necessary because if other investors have also found the pattern, they will buy in anticipation of a rise in the stock price; this buying surge then leads to a change in the pattern you found.

Imagine the following scenario: You think I am really good at finding patterns, and I tell you that I am 100% confident I have found a pattern in the price movement of GE stock. Then I tell you that the pattern I have found indicates GE will double next Monday. You assume you should buy GE now and wait until Monday to take your profits. But if *everyone* knows GE will double by Monday, GE will actually double *today* because everyone will buy it immediately. The pattern has been destroyed, because everyone is buying GE now instead of when they would have normally bought it in the future. So for the pattern to persist, only a few investors can be aware of the pattern; otherwise, the pattern will not continue. What are the odds there is a pattern movement of a stock price that leads to above-market returns—and that you are the only one who has found it?

The research of bright individuals who are trying to earn PhDs in economics or finance, or are trying to publish in academic journals, has all found that the price movement of stocks is basically a random walk.[43] If you see a drunk person walking on the street, you know where he has walked in the past, but you have no idea where the next step will take him. In the case of the stock market, you have a 50% chance the stock will move up in price and a 50% chance it will move down. You know where the stock price has been in the past, but that gives you no clue where the price will go in the future—just like the drunk on the street.

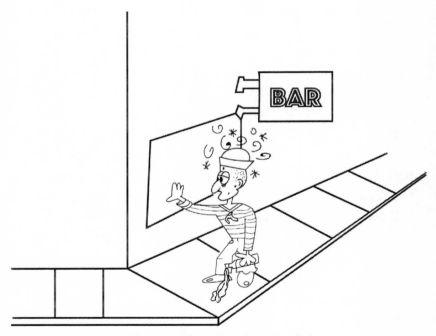

I have no idea where he is headed.

The weak form of the efficient market hypothesis states that past price movements have no bearing on how stocks will perform in the future. Technical analysts are looking for patterns in price movements of stocks; hence, if the weak form of the efficient market hypothesis holds (and the evidence supports that it does), it means technical analysis does not work in identifying stocks that will outperform a buy-and-hold strategy. Just like a drunk who is walking down the street, you know where the stock price has been, but you have no idea where it is going.

FUNDAMENTAL ANALYSIS/SEMI-STRONG FORM OF THE EFFICIENT MARKET HYPOTHESIS

When speaking about an efficient stock market, most economists (including me) are referring to the semi-strong form of the efficient market hypothesis. You are about to learn what this means. Yes, this will be on the exam.

The vast majority of analysts whose job it is to find undervalued stocks use some form of fundamental analysis. A substantial part of my investment course is spent covering the issues faced by analysts who use fundamental analysis to evaluate stocks. The theory and the mathematics become complicated enough that they can drive even very good undergraduate students to spend hours in the library, trying to comprehend the intricacies of fundamental analysis (at least, just before the final exam).

Although I am tempted to include one of the mathematical formulas used in fundamental analysis in this book, it would serve no useful purpose, except to show how complicated the math can become. For that, you can use your imagination. The *goal* of fundamental analysis, however, is simple: to find the intrinsic value of a stock (i.e., what the stock is really worth). An analyst does that by attempting to find the present value of all future cash flows to a shareholder of a particular company. The result of this calculation becomes the intrinsic value of the company. Choosing what stocks to invest in is now easy: Buy stocks that are selling for substantially less than the calculated intrinsic value.

Are you sure I need to understand this just to invest in the stock market?

Fundamental analysts must determine the current worth of all future dividends, or as economists would say, the present value of *all* future cash flows to the shareholder. This is the intrinsic value of a stock.

Those of you who are still awake should ask, "You have to predict the future cash dividends using fundamental analysis?" The answer is "yes."

Then you might ask, "For how long?" The answer is "forever."

"Is there anything else?"

Yes. You also need to calculate the correct risk profile of the company (i.e., the correct discount rate).

Now you understand why you did not become a stock analyst; all that is required is that you accurately predict the future cash flows of a company to infinity and beyond. Any mistake predicting future dividends or the correct discount rate will yield an incorrect intrinsic value calculation. Garbage in, garbage out. Could it be the stock is correctly priced but your calculation of the intrinsic value is wrong? If you decide the stock is truly undervalued, you will be betting against the wisdom of the crowd.

The previous explanation lays out the bad news about fundamental analysis and why so many undergraduates avoid investment courses like the plague: its *complexity*. There is good news, however: You do not need to calculate the present value of all future cash flows or use any other mathematical formula to be a savvy investor. This is because so many analysts are working around the clock using fundamental analysis to find undervalued stocks. By constantly looking for undervalued/overvalued stocks, they have driven all stocks to their intrinsic value. If there is a stock that is undervalued/overvalued, they will buy/sell it until it reaches its fair value. Thus, you can be assured that all stocks are fairly priced; you can become a free rider. Or as we would say in an investment class, all public information has been discounted into the price of all stocks.

This leads to a quandary: Fundamental analysis will not work for *you* because the professionals on Wall Street are using it so effectively. They have found the "bargain" stocks and have driven the price to the intrinsic value. They have done the work for you and have told you the correct answer of what the true price of a stock should be: its current price. The fundamental analysts do the work, and you reap the benefits of their work. Free lunch time!

The semi-strong form of the efficient market hypothesis states that at any point in time, all stock prices reflect all public information available about the stock. If you are to make above-market return, you must consistently predict the future better than the best minds on Wall Street. Many have tried, and almost all have failed. If the semi-strong form of the efficient market hypothesis holds, then fundamental analysis will not work to help you find undervalued stocks because all stocks are fairly priced. Most independent researchers who have nothing to sell think the stock market is basically semi-strong efficient. Some may argue that there are pockets of inefficiencies in the stock market, but these pockets are small at best.

STRONG FORM OF THE EFFICIENT MARKET HYPOTHESIS

The semi-strong form of the efficient market hypothesis states that no public information will help analysts select under-valued securities. This means fundamental analysis is no better than technical analysis in enabling investors to find undervalued stocks. The strong form of the efficient market hypothesis takes it one step further by stating that absolutely nothing that is known (or even knowable) about a company will benefit an investor (i.e., no public or private information will help an investor earn above-average returns in the market). This leads to the conclusion that even insider information will not allow an investor to beat the market, which we know is false, as there are numerous historical examples of insiders profiting from private information. Of course, they often end up in jail. The point, however, is that the strong form of the efficient market hypothesis is wrong.

THE CROWD

The theory of the collective wisdom of a group of analysts (i.e., the semi-strong form of the efficient market hypothesis) can be illustrated by what English scientist Francis Galton found in the early 1900s, when he discovered that the collective wisdom of many is more accurate than the wisdom of a few experts.[44] Galton made his discovery at a livestock convention, where a crowd of almost 800 people was asked to guess the correct weight of a butchered ox. Although there was wide variation among the guesses, the average of the guesses of the 800 people was within one pound of the correct weight. This amazing result has been extended to many other situations. In 2004, James Surowiecki wrote *The Wisdom of Crowds: Why the Many Are Smarter than the Few and How Collective Wisdom Shapes Business, Economies, Societies and Nations.* In his book, Surowiecki argues that the aggregation of information in groups and the predications that result from that aggregation are better than could have been made by any single member of the group. His central thesis is that a diverse group of individuals making independent decisions is likely to make better decisions and predictions than would be made by a few experts. The implication for the stock market is that the thousands of investors who invest each day will prove to be better than any single expert or group of experts in predicting the intrinsic value of a stock. Individual stock analysts cannot beat the wisdom of the crowd of market investors. In a debate on active versus passive management, Rex Sinquefield, a leading financial expert, said:

> It is well to consider, briefly, the connection between the socialists and the active managers. I believe they are cut from the same cloth. What links them is a disbelief or skepticism about the efficacy of market prices in gathering and conveying information. ... So

who still believes markets don't work? Apparently it is only the North Koreans, Cubans and the active managers.[45]

MANAGED MUTUAL FUNDS

One of the most compelling pieces of evidence that supports the premise that the stock market is semi-strong efficient is the record of the mutual fund industry. By law, mutual funds must publicly disclose what return they have earned. How have the actively managed mutual funds performed compared to an index or an average? Just by chance, one might expect 50% of the actively managed funds to beat the appropriate index. According to an S&P Dow Jones Indices scorecard, however, a staggering 76% of active large-cap fund managers failed to beat the index in 2015. Nearly 89% of fund managers underperformed the index over the five years prior to 2015, and 82% underperformed over the ten years prior to 2015.[46] This means that most active mutual fund managers cannot earn their keep; they cannot compete with the index after they pay themselves. This is exactly what the semi-strong form of the efficient market hypothesis would predict.

Shouldn't we invest in one of the approximately 10% to 15% who *did* beat the index? Now we are back to the two-handed economist, and the answer is, it depends. As I pointed out in the Introduction, there are thousands of mutual funds, and if there is a 50/50 chance you can beat the market by simply being lucky, you will have some who beat the market ten years in a row—simply by being lucky. No one has yet found a way to sort the truly gifted from the lucky. And even after you are sure you have found the Holy Grail, is that portfolio manager still working for that particular mutual fund? If he or she is, others will have discovered the genius, too, and the fund will have grown by several times. Then the relevant question becomes whether that manager can do what was done when the fund was much smaller. When a mutual fund has more assets under management, the fund managers need to find even more undervalued companies to put in their portfolios. Their success has turned a very difficult problem into a colossal nightmare.

I hope it has become abundantly clear that it is difficult, if not impossible, to find a mutual fund manager who will consistently beat a market index. The managers who are flying high for a year or two will likely become next year's goats. As I have said before, it is usually better to pick a managed mutual fund in the bottom quartile in terms of return than one in the top quartile because of the phenomenon known as *regression to the mean*.

Most of the trades in today's stock market are made by institutional money, including mutual funds. Not all of this invested money can earn above-average returns. By definition, everyone in the stock market must earn average returns, minus any expenses. Just to earn the *average* return, mutual fund managers must beat the market by the amount they are charging to manage the fund. Unless Wall Street is in Lake Wobegon— where everyone is above average—it is impossible, due to expense charges, for most mutual fund managers to earn even average returns.

WARREN BUFFETT

When one discusses an efficient stock market, one should talk about the elephant in the room: Warren Buffett. A $10,000 investment in 1965 in Warren Buffett's Berkshire Hathaway company stock would have grown to be worth nearly $30 million forty years later. That is about sixty times more than you would have made if you had invested $10,000 in the S&P 500 index. Mr. Buffett once said, "I'd be a bum on the street with a tin cup if the markets were always efficient."[47]

In hindsight, it is easy to see that Mr. Buffett has extraordinary talents; his record over time is nothing short of remarkable. If you can find a young Mr. Buffett, then you should invest all your money with that person, and come 2055, you can enjoy $30 million for each $10,000 you invested.

It is not clear, however, that Berkshire Hathaway has done as well in the past few years as it did in the early years of the fund. The returns for Berkshire Hathaway during the fifteen years ending in June 2013 trailed several index funds. A headline in *Fortune* magazine stated, "Warren Buffett's Investing Successors Blew It in 2014." Todd Combs, one of Buffett's handpicked successors, missed the mark by the most. His portfolio fell 0.3%, while the S&P was up 11%—before dividends. Weschler, another of Buffett's handpicked successors, had a portfolio that was up 6.7%, which means he also trailed the S&P Index.

Although the long-term record of Berkshire Hathaway is remarkable, it may not sustain that past record in the future. Buffett is well into his eighties, and the size of the fund is enormous. Can the fund accomplish the same things it did when it was a small and agile? The jury is still out.

I think it is enlightening to examine what Mr. Buffett has told the trustees of his estate: "Invest in index funds." In a recent annual letter to Berkshire shareholders, Buffett wrote:

> My advice to the trustees couldn't be more simple: Put 10% of the cash in short-term government bonds and 90% in a very low-cost S&P 500 index fund. ... I believe the trust's long-term results from this policy will be superior to those attained by most investors—whether pension funds, institutions, or individuals—who employ high-fee managers.[48]

For several years, Buffett has been touting index funds as a good investment vehicle and has made it perfectly clear that he considers index funds to be the best investment for his estate. What is striking about the above quotation is not that he favors index funds but that he does not want his executor to keep money in Berkshire Hathaway. It appears that even Warren Buffett considers finding the next Warren Buffett impossible.

In 2008, Buffett wagered $1 million that over a ten-year period, an S&P 500 Index fund could beat five actively managed funds chosen by Protégé Partners, a prominent New York asset management firm. The $1 million will be donated to charity (you can make these kinds of bets when you are worth several billion dollars). In mid-2016, Mr. Buffett's S&P 500 Index Fund was up 65.7%, while the actively managed funds were up 21.9%. Unless something very unusual happens, it appears Mr. Buffett will win the bet. Buffett put his money behind his long-held argument that "experts" do no better than the stock market as a whole. The Francis Galton crowd, who guessed the correct weight of the butchered ox, seems to be working in the stock market. Do you still want to buy an actively managed fund when Warren Buffett is betting on an index fund?

INDEX FUNDS

As I pointed out earlier, there is a classification of mutual funds known as *index funds*. These funds do not try to *beat* an index, but rather try to *match* an index by simply buying all the stocks in that index. One of the main advantages index funds have over managed mutual funds is that they can charge lower fees because they do not have to hire expensive portfolio managers. This lower cost structure allows index funds to pass along more of the returns from the stock market to shareholders. In some cases, the management fees for an actively managed fund can be twenty times or more higher than the fees charged by an index fund.

The efficient market hypothesis leads to the conclusion that all stocks are fairly priced; hence, no one can beat the market average. If you cannot earn more than the market return, why pay a mutual fund a high fee? Over time, these excess fees can mean tens of thousands of dollars in lost income to the shareholder. If the market is up 10% per year over the long run, and you pay someone 1% to manage your portfolio, then your net return will be 9%. On the other hand (yes, I am a two-handed economist), you can buy an index fund and pay only 0.05% in fees; thus, you will receive a 9.95% return. If you make an initial investment of $10,000 and leave it in the account for thirty years, the difference can be very large in the end.

Initial deposit	Number of years invested	Average annual return compounded monthly	End balance
$10,000	30 years	9.95%	$195,445
$10,000	30 years	9.00%	$147,306

As you can see, the result is that over thirty years, you will have paid excess management fees of $48,139 ($195,445 - $147,306), or 4.8 times more than your initial deposit.

Fortunately, there are index funds that charge fees as low as 0.05% (0.0005). If you invest $10,000 in such a fund, the charge for managing your money is $5 during the first year, or approximately the cost of one Starbucks specialty drink. Even in the thirtieth year when you have $195,445 invested, your fees would be less than $100 for the year.

As I mentioned in the Introduction, an index mutual fund has two related advantages over an actively managed mutual fund: stocks are traded infrequently (i.e., lower turnover rates), and index funds are more tax-efficient. When a stock is traded, there are costs (including a broker's and trader's fee) associated with those trades. The fewer times you trade, the fewer times you have to pay those fees.

Because they are trying to *match*, not beat, the average, the index fund managers simply buy and hold the stocks in the index. Index funds only have to buy and sell stocks when the stocks in an index change. The average holding period for an index fund can be as long as ten years, whereas for actively managed funds, the period may be as short as six months. These savings on trading costs can have a significant impact on returns over the long-term.

Because of their low turnover of stocks in the portfolio, index funds are also tax-efficient. This is important because each time a mutual fund *sells* a stock and makes a profit on that sale, it must report the profit to the IRS. The mutual fund must pass this tax liability along to the shareholder, requiring the shareholder to pay tax on the capital gain. Index funds trade infrequently; thus, they do not have to pass on as many capital gains as actively managed mutual funds. In a retirement account, this is not a problem, because realized capital gains are tax deferred. Outside of retirement accounts, however, this is an important issue.

SO HOW DOES THE MARKET WORK?

As we have seen, the conventional wisdom among academics is that the semi-strong form of the efficient market hypothesis describes how the stock market actually works. The implication is that technical and fundamental analysis will not help you—or anyone else—find undervalued stocks. The best strategy, then, is to buy index mutual funds.

Although I think that for the most part, the semi-strong form of the efficient market hypothesis is correct, I believe there are some cracks in the hypothesis. This is good news for those of you who want to do more than just buy one index fund.

These small pockets of inefficiency will not lead to great riches, but they might allow you to earn a better-than-average market return over the long run. If you want to do better than the market, you have to go where the big boys/girls do not play. Because professional investment managers have so much money to invest, in general they cannot play the small-cap game. It is simply not worth large investors' time to hunt for undervalued small-cap stocks; due to the size of small companies, large investors cannot put enough money into any one company to justify the time and expense of looking for undervalued small-cap companies. Since these stocks are not being followed by as many analysts, however, there is a higher probability you can find a stock that is truly undervalued.

The second potential pocket of inefficiency is in stocks that are out of favor with the majority of analysts. These stocks are often characterized as "value stocks" (contrasted with growth stocks). Remember, if you are going to beat Wall Street, you cannot run with the crowd; you must be a contrarian. When the "smart" money is moving away from a stock, it *might* be a good time for you to move in—and vice versa. The trick is to sort out the real dogs from the diamonds in the rough.

If I were the only one who thought this, you might be skeptical, but two of the most famous academics in the investment field—Professors Eugene Fama and Kenneth French—wrote a paper that has become the most widely cited paper in financial economics.[49] Their three-factor model found that small company stocks received higher returns than large company stocks and that value stocks also received higher returns than growth stocks. When they tested this hypothesis on historical data, they found that stocks with these characteristics yielded higher returns than would have been predicted by looking only at their risk characteristics. In future chapters, when I suggest portfolios, I will use the Fama-French three-factor model to construct some of the more aggressive portfolios. This strategy will not win you instant riches, but it may help you earn more than a market return.

MARKET TIMING

As I suggested in the beginning of this chapter, you only need to follow one rule when investing in the stock market: Buy low, sell high. In general, individual investors do not follow this rule. When the stock market is doing well and everyone is making money in the market, individuals tend to buy; when pessimism is everywhere and the market is falling, they tend to sell. Consequently, they are buying high and selling low. I will argue that the correct strategy for you is to buy and hold through thick and thin.

It is impossible to be a market timer. Many have tried, and I know of no one who has been consistently successful. Successful market timing requires two correct decisions: when to get out of the market and when to get back in. Both decisions must be correct if you are going to be truly successful. How often does a market timer have to be right to beat an index? In 1975, Nobel Laureate William Sharpe wrote an article titled "Likely Gains from Market Timing."[50] His research determined that you must be accurate 74% of the time in order to outperform a passive portfolio. When you examine the record of self-proclaimed market timers, you find that none were able to match the benchmark set by Sharpe. The empirical evidence is clear that market timing has not worked for those who have tried.

Being right most of the time when utilizing a market timing strategy is not good enough if you want to be a successful market investor. Immense stock market gains and losses are concentrated into just a few trading days. Missing only a few days can have a dramatic impact on returns. For the twenty-year period from 1994–2013, the following chart shows how missing the five, ten, and forty best days in the S&P 500 affected the market return.

S&P 500 ANNUAL RETURN 1994–2013

Annual return	Annual return if you miss the five best days	Annual return if you miss the ten best days	Annual return if you miss the forty best days
9.2%	7.0%	3.0%	-1.9%

There were approximately 5,000 trading days during this twenty-year period. If you missed the forty best days, you would have gone from making 9.2% per year to making -1.9%. Those forty days represent less than 1% of all trading days. Still want to try market timing?

To be a successful market timer requires you to miss the worst days, which are equally concentrated and just as difficult to identify. If you had missed the forty worst days during the period of 1994–2013, your return would have been more than nine times better than the return earned by investors who stayed the course during the entire twenty years. Unless you can anticipate the 1% of days that are going to be the worst performing, however, you are not going to get the nine-times-better return. This excess return is what is so alluring about market timing. To be truly successful, however, you must be invested in the market on the great days and completely out of the market on the worst days. All you have to do is predict the future with a high degree of accuracy. No one has been able to consistently buy at the absolute bottom of the market and sell at the absolute high.

To further make this point, University of Michigan Professor H. Nejat Seyhun analyzed 7,802 trading days for the thirty-one-year period spanning 1963–1993. He concluded that just ninety days during that period generated 95% of all the years' market gains—an average of just *three days per year*.[51]

Unfortunately, we are not playing a game of horseshoes, where being close would allow you to win the timing game. Instead, you have to be near perfect to beat a buy-and-hold strategy. In fact, if you had missed those ninety days mentioned above, you would have had almost no gains to show for being in the market the other 7,712 days.

Market timing has not worked in the past, and it will not work in the future. If you are going to be a successful investor, you must use a buy-and-hold strategy, which requires you to be in the market when it is going down and to view declines in the market as opportunities to buy low.

DOLLAR-COST AVERAGING

One of my favorite "gotcha" questions I ask my students is this: If you invest $1,000 today when a stock is selling for $10 and then invest $1,000 a year from today when the same stock is selling for $5, what is the average cost per share of your portfolio holdings?

Almost every time, an ambitious student will respond, "$7.50."

This is a reasonable answer (($10 + 5)/2), but it is wrong. $7.50 would be the correct answer if you had bought the same number of *shares* the second time, not invested the same amount of *money*.

In the first transaction, you bought 100 shares at $1,000/$10, and in the second transaction, you bought *200 shares* at $1,000/$5. Hence, the correct answer is $2,000/300, or $6.67 per share. That is the magic of dollar-cost averaging. The average price over time is $7.50, but the average cost of the stocks you purchased is $6.67.

Dollar-cost averaging allows you to buy more shares with the same investment dollars when the price of a stock has fallen. This is, of course, the first rule of smart investing: Buy low. When individuals ask me for advice about what they should do after receiving a windfall, I tell them to spread their money into the stock market over a period of time so that in hindsight, they do not find that they bought at precisely the wrong time (i.e., when the market was approaching a high). I tell these individuals not to be a "plunger"; instead, put the same amount of money into the market on a set schedule (for example, once a month), regardless of what direction the market is moving. This will allow the individuals to take advantage of dollar-cost averaging.

If you are investing for the long run, which is exactly what you should be doing if you are putting your money into the stock market, you should actually hope the market does not go up while you are buying shares. Only when you *sell* do you hope the market hits a record high.

In his 1997 Chairman's Letter to the shareholders of Berkshire Hathaway, Warren Buffett stated this principle perfectly:

> A short quiz: if you plan to eat hamburgers throughout your life and are not a cattle producer, should you wish for higher or lower prices of beef? Likewise, if you are going to buy a car from time to time but are not an auto manufacturer, should you prefer higher or lower car prices? These questions, of course, answer themselves.
>
> But now for the final exam: if you expect to be a net saver during the next five years, should you hope for a higher or lower stock market during that period? Many investors get this one wrong. Even though they are going to be net buyers of stock for many years to come, they are elated when stock prices rise

and depressed when they fall. In effect, they rejoice because prices have risen for the "hamburgers" they will soon be buying. This reaction makes no sense. Only those who will be sellers of equities in the near future should be happy at seeing stocks rise. Prospective purchasers should much prefer sinking prices.[52]

Dollar-cost averaging will not save you from paper market losses when the market takes a substantial downturn. The trick is to have the nerve to continue buying when the market is drifting downward. The market may be down 10% this month, but you have to buy and buy again if it drops another 10%. If you do not buy stocks when the market is down, you will lose the benefit of buying some of your shares at a reduced price (i.e., buying low). Buying stocks when the market is down is not easy; the conventional wisdom is that the market will continue heading down. But you will be a winner when the market starts moving up again.

Dollar-cost averaging will give you this bargain: The average price you paid per share for stocks in your portfolio will be lower than the average price at the time you bought the shares (in my example, $6.67 vs. $7.50). You now know the answer to the "gotcha" question, and you know why it will allow investors to buy shares at a lower average price than one might initially expect.

The easiest way for me to take advantage of dollar-cost-averaging is to set up an automatic investment plan with a mutual fund company. Every week, regardless of what the stock market is doing, my mutual fund company adds the same dollar amount to my portfolio of mutual funds. There is strong evidence that dollar-cost averaging and buy-and-hold will allow you to do better than most investors in the stock market. It has worked for me, and it should work for you.

SUMMARY

This chapter was dedicated to convincing you that the stock market is semi-strong efficient (i.e., that all public information is reflected in stock prices). Almost all academics subscribe to some form of the semi-strong efficient market hypothesis. These individuals have nothing to sell but are striving to determine how stocks really behave in the market. Remember, if you are going to buy individual stocks or hire an active mutual fund manager to buy individual stocks for you, you are betting against the collective wisdom of thousands of very smart people who work extremely hard to find undervalued stocks.

I have also tried to argue that timing when to get into and out of the market is a futile exercise. In fact, there is strong evidence that individual investors lose a significant percentage of their potential gains by buying and selling at precisely the wrong time. There is evidence that the typical investor loses 2% or more per year by buying high and selling low. The best defense against making such a mistake is to do dollar-cost averaging: Buy the same dollar amount at a set interval or sell the same dollar amount at a set interval.

Given what we just covered, here are the dos and don'ts for investors:

- **Do not try to pick undervalued stocks**. The stock market is semi-strong efficient.
- **Do not buy an actively managed mutual fund**. Their returns do not justify the higher cost of investing.
- **Do not try to do market timing**. Unless you are perfect at timing, this strategy will not work.
- **Do not pick a managed mutual fund based on recent performance**. Those near the top in terms of returns tend to regress.

- **Do use index mutual funds**. Low cost allows you to earn market return.
- **Do have a plan for set periodic buying of index mutual funds**. This will allow you to gain the advantage of dollar-cost averaging.

Armed with the knowledge you have gained in this and previous chapters, it is now time to cover the specifics of where to invest. Wall Street, here we come!

CHAPTER 5

RULES OF THE ROAD

Several years ago, Wausau Insurance Company ran an advertisement on TV that showed an auditorium filled with what appeared to be company executives. The person who introduced the keynote speaker described him as the "world expert in business insurance" and said he would convey to everyone in the audience everything they needed to know about business insurance. The speaker walked to the podium, unfolded his notes, and looked out into the crowd. He hesitated and said only one word: "Wausau." After picking up his notes, he walked off the stage. There was initial silence from the crowd, followed by enthusiastic applause.

I cannot give you a one-word prescription for successful investing, but if I were giving the Wausau investment speech, I would unfold my notes and say, "Cost and allocation." As I explained in the Introduction, these are the two variables that you, as an investor, can control. I am confident that understanding the importance of these two variables and effectively controlling them will allow you to compete with Warren Buffett for the $1 million prize and handily beat those five investment managers selected by Protégé Partners.

In previous chapters, I tried to convince you that at any given point in time, all stocks are fairly priced (i.e., the stock market is semi-strong efficient). If this is true, then neither you nor anyone else can outperform the stock market. If no one can outperform the market, then the lower the cost of managing your portfolio, the better the return you will earn. For the long-run success of your portfolio, it is important to keep costs as low as possible.

The other variable you can control is allocation. Your allocation decision will determine the *risk* you have undertaken and the *return* you are likely to earn over the long run. This allocation decision basically comes down to what percentage of money to allocate to risky assets (e.g., stocks) and what percentage to allocate to a less risky investment (e.g., bonds).

Remember how important it is to concentrate on the variables you *do* control: the total cost you pay to maintain your portfolio and the allocation among the various investment options. If you control these variables in an intelligent way, you will maximize the return you will earn from your portfolio.

RULE 1: KEEP COST AS LOW AS POSSIBLE

Rule number one is to keep cost as low as possible when you construct your portfolio. After reading the previous chapters, this rule should not surprise you. In general, people expect a better commodity when they pay a higher price for a product. When you pay more for a car, you expect a better car; when you pay more for a house, you expect a better house and/or a better location. The stock market may be the exception to this rule. Because overwhelming empirical evidence demonstrates that the stock market is semi-strong efficient, it can be argued that if you are paying for investment advice on how to beat the stock market, you are getting nothing better than what you would get if you bought snake oil to cure cancer.

What may seem like a very small difference in management fees can add up to a substantial sum of money over long periods. For example, if you could put aside $150 per month and earn 10% per year for thirty years—or earn the same 10% but pay an advisor 1%—you would have the following payouts:

$150 PER MONTH, 30 YEARS AT 10%
9% WITH AN ADVISOR

Payment per month	Total set aside 30 years	Net returns	Balance after 30 years
$150	$54,000	10%	$342,000
$150	$54,000	9%	$277,000

The bottom line is that over thirty years, you would have paid $65,000 for the advice you received, resulting in having about 20% less value in your account. Fortunately, there are excellent mutual funds that charge very low management fees and can save you almost all of this $65,000.

I am always amused when someone tells me they are only paying 1% for their investment advice. What they actually mean is that they are paying 1% of their gross portfolio value to the advisor both when the portfolio increases in value *and* when it declines. This does not sound too bad—until you start to think about other ways you might view this 1% charge. Remember, you might reasonably expect an approximate 10% return on your stock portfolio over time. That means the person giving you advice is taking 10% (1%/10%) of your gain—without taking any of the risk. Put another way: *You* take all the risk, and the advisor takes 10% of your rewards.

A third way of evaluating this fee is to remember that you could receive a 10% return by simply buying an index fund. Let's assume you have Superman as an investment advisor; he can leap tall buildings in a single bound and can earn excess returns in the stock market. In fact, he can get you 11% per year on your portfolio when the average market return is 10% (this would be a super-human feat!). This means that after his fees, you would receive 10%, just as you would have from an index fund. Superman charged you 100% of the extra return he earned for you. If he is Superman Lite and only makes 10.5% (which would still be a remarkable excess return), then he charged you 200% of the extra return he earned for you, and you would have earned 9.5% vs. the 10% from the stock market. Still think 1% sounds cheap?

Over long periods of time, high fees can have an extraordinary effect on the value of a portfolio. Consider a target-date mutual fund (the date on the fund is when you might retire) that is offered in a 403(b) plan and has a 1.11% advisor fee without any fee waivers. Vanguard offers a comparable fund that charges 0.18% (see chart below). If you earn a gross return of 10% on the Vanguard fund for thirty-five years and have set aside $1,000 per month in your retirement account, at the end of thirty-five years, the balance of your account would be approximately $3.7 million. If you set aside the same $1,000 per month in a target-date mutual fund that has higher expenses and earns the same 10% before the higher expenses are taken out of the account, at the end of thirty-five years, the balance of your retirement account would be approximately $2.9 million. Over that thirty-five-year period, the extra fee would cost you approximately $800,000.

THIRTY-FIVE-YEAR SET-ASIDE
10% GROSS RETURN

Monthly set-aside	Total set-aside over thirty-five years	Net return	Ending balance
$1,000	$420,000	10% - 0.18 % = 9.82%	$3,654,305
$1,000	$420,000	10% - 1.11% = 8.89%	$2,882,658

It should now be very clear why it is important to concentrate on the fees charged by mutual funds or investment advisors. An advisor would have to be very special to justify $800,000 of extra fees.

Currently, there are many different index funds that try to match the S&P 500 Index. Not all of these funds are created equal; some have very high fees, and some have fees as low as 0.05%. It is very important to know the expense ratio for any mutual fund you are considering adding to your portfolio. I can think of no reason why anyone should buy an index fund with a high expense ratio.

In summary, if I were doing the "Wausau speech," one of the words I would say is "costs." Keep costs as low as possible; anything over 1/2 of 1% is too high. Every mutual fund I own has costs under 0.20%, with some of the expense ratios as low as 0.05%. This is a message mutual fund portfolio managers do not want you to hear because the money you save could have helped pay for their homes in the Hamptons. Millions of dollars go to portfolio managers—dollars that could be retained by individual investors. Keep your share of investment gains by buying low-cost mutual funds.

COROLLARY I TO RULE 1

Not only should you keep costs as low as possible but you should also start saving for long-term projects (retirement, college expenses for children, etc.) as soon as you can. *It is never too early to start saving.* To illustrate, assume Jane starts saving for retirement at age twenty-five. She sets aside $1,000 per month and earns 10% per year. At age thirty-five, she decides to stop adding to this account but keeps the money invested at a 10% annual return for the next thirty years. At age thirty-five, Tarzan decides it is time for him to start saving and tries to catch up with Jane's retirement savings. He puts aside $1,500 per month for the next *thirty* years. Like Jane, he earns a 10% return on his account.

Jane set aside $120,000 over ten years, and Tarzan set aside $540,000 over thirty years. When they both reach age sixty-five, Jane will have approximately $4 million in her account, and Tarzan will have approximately $3.4 million. Jane invested for ten years and let that result compound for another thirty years, while Tarzan invested 50% more per month than Jane for thirty years. Even then, he could not catch up. He had a significantly lower amount of money in his portfolio: $600,000 less than Jane.

Retirement Investment For
Tarzan and Jane
Assuming a 10% per year return

	Total Dollars Invested	Number of years putting money in the account	Approximate ending value
Jane	$120,000	10	$4.0 million
Tarzan	$540,000	30	$3.4 million

No matter how many times I see this result, it still amazes me. This is the power of compounding! Moral to the story: Start saving as soon as you can.

How can you earn more money than me?
I invested 4.5X more money!

COROLLARY II TO RULE 1

Dollar-cost averaging, which was covered in the previous chapter, is another way to keep the overall cost of investing under control. Although dollar-cost averaging does not directly affect the cost you pay for advice, it does have an impact on the average price you pay for shares of a mutual fund. The important thing to remember about dollar-cost averaging is that you must have the discipline to buy when the market is going down (i.e., to buy low). Rarely, if ever, will you be able to buy at the absolute lowest point in the market, but you can keep the average cost of shares down by buying when stock prices are down.

RULE 1 SUMMARY

There are three elements of Rule 1:

- **Keep the costs on your account as low as possible.** As a rule of thumb, do not pay more fees than 0.5% for a mutual fund. As a starting point, I use 0.2% as a reasonable fee for a mutual fund. You can find some very good alternatives that charge as low as 0.05%.

- **Start saving as soon as possible for future expenditures.** If you are intending to use the money in the next five years, the stock market may not be the place to put your money. I use this five-year rule because of the volatility of the stock market. For anything shorter than five years, it is probably best to use a short-term investment vehicle like a bank savings account to avoid the volatility of the stock market. If, however, your need for money is more than five years into the future, let compounding work for you by starting early to invest for long-term projects.

- **Take advantage of dollar-cost averaging.** This is easy to say but hard to execute because it requires you to buy when the stock market is down. Remember Warren Buffett's analogy about buying hamburgers? In the accumulation phase of your life, you should wish for the stock market to remain low. Only when you are selling should you wish for the market to reach highs.

RULE 2: FIND THE CORRECT ALLOCATION

The most important decision you will make when investing is *how to allocate your money* among the various investment options. This allocation decision will determine the level of risk you will assume and the expected rate of return of your portfolio. No other factor has as much influence on determining the rate of return of your portfolio. Most empirical studies have shown that the allocation among various asset classes in your portfolio will be the major driver—an astonishing 94%—of the long-run return you can expect.[53] It is extremely important you understand the risk you have taken with your allocation decision, the implication for return, and the volatility you might have to endure. Never let anyone talk you into more risk than you can tolerate. The correct level of risk is sometimes referred to as the *sleep-down point*: If the risk level you have in your portfolio causes you to toss and turn in bed at night but allows you to sleep, the risk you have taken is at the highest level allowable. If you cannot sleep, however, then you have undertaken too much risk and need to reduce that risk in your portfolio.

Please back off some risk in the stock market so we can sleep.

If you buy only US short-term treasury bills (T-bills), both your risk and your return will be very low. In fact, short-term treasury bills are considered by most individuals to have zero risk, but over long periods of time, they also have yielded zero *real* return (i.e., the return after inflation). On the other hand, if you buy small-cap stocks with borrowed money, you will have taken on a great deal of risk. With this small-cap investment, you can expect a high return over the long run, but there may be extended periods where you have low or negative returns. For most of us, the risk we can tolerate is somewhere between these two extremes.

This is worth repeating: The *allocation* of your assets among the various asset classes will be the main driver of what you can expect your return to be over the long run.

One of the more frequent sentiments I hear when discussing investment options with individuals is that they want a very high return and no risk. Yes, they want a free lunch. Don't we all? If it were that easy, however, I would not have to write this book, and we could all sleep well at night knowing our portfolios would never lose any money. Unfortunately, the investment world does not work that way. In order to receive a higher return (i.e., a "good"), you must take on more risk (i.e., a "bad").

The allocation decision you make regarding what assets you buy will determine the level of risk in your portfolio. Too much risk, and you will not be able to sleep—and you may panic-sell at precisely the wrong time. Too little risk, and your return will be less than is optimum for you.

In finance, standard deviation is often used as a proxy for risk. If you do not remember what standard deviation is, do not worry. Just remember that the larger the standard deviation, the more the price of your stock will deviate from its average return (i.e., fall short of earning the average return in the short run). A standard deviation of zero means you will receive the same return every year (i.e., there will be no deviation from the average).

Put simply, the larger the standard deviation, the larger the deviation from the average.

SUMMARY STATISTICS FOR RETURN AND RISK
1926–2009

Investment options	Return	Standard deviation
Small-cap stocks	11.9%	32.8%
Large-cap stocks	9.8%	20.5%
Long-term corporate bonds	5.4%	8.3%
US Treasury bills	3.7%	3.1%

Source: Ibbotson Associates

From the above chart, it is clear that over a long period of time, the more risk (i.e., higher standard deviation) an investor tolerated, the higher the return that individual earned. Inflation was 3.0% during this period; hence, T-bills had very little real return but had the least amount of risk. Over the same period, 68% (or one standard deviation) of the time, the return on small-cap stocks was between 44.7% and -20.9%, while 95% (or two standard deviation) of the time, the return was between 77.5% and -58.7%. We can all live with the 44.7% and 77.5%, but can you live with -20.9% and -58.7%? If you can't stand the "heat" from these kinds of swings in returns, you will need to get out of the "kitchen" and back off the risk you have taken.

Finding your risk tolerance is not an easy task. Investors can assess their degree of risk tolerance by taking one of a number of different risk-tolerance questionnaires that can be found on the Internet. Although I find these questionnaires of limited value, they *will* give you some idea of what kinds of things might affect your tolerance for risk. It is important that you do not allow anyone to talk you into taking on more risk than you can tolerate, and you understand both what kinds of returns you can expect for the risk you take and what potential losses you might encounter for a given level of risk.

Economists divide stock market risk into two distinct kinds: systematic risk (which is associated with the general trends of the market) and unsystematic risk (which is uniquely associated with a particular stock).

When the economy is going through a difficult time, where unemployment and/or inflation are high and the GDP is stagnant or falling, all stocks tend to move down together. This is an example of systematic risk. If you invest in the stock market, you are in the "system," and thus, you are going to experience systematic risk. Practically speaking, there is no way to avoid this kind of risk—except to stay out of the stock market.

The second kind of risk, unsystematic risk, is associated with a particular stock and not with the stock market in general. For example, a particular stock you own may have been hit by a massive lawsuit, a merger that went bad, an unanticipated decline in earnings, etc. These events are associated with a particular stock and are not germane to the general stock market. Unsystematic risk by definition is random and unpredictable. Of course, such random events can also be positive (e.g., a new and unexpected contract to sell a company's product, a breakthrough in technology, a friendly merger, etc.).

If you own just one stock, you will have both systematic and unsystematic risk associated with your portfolio, but as you add stocks, you will have some stocks with positive unsystematic risk and some with negative unsystematic risk. When you have a sufficient number of stocks in your portfolio, the positive unsystematic risk will cancel out the negative unsystematic risk. Unsystematic risk is something you do not want in your portfolio of stocks; it adds to the volatility of a portfolio.

The question then becomes how many stocks you need to own to eliminate unsystematic risk. The empirical evidence demonstrates that if you own approximately thirty stocks, your unsystematic risk will approach zero. Since unsystematic risk can be eliminated, you will not receive a higher return for any unsystematic risk that remains in your portfolio. In other words, you will not be compensated for taking on risk you should have avoided (i.e., for being dumb). Throughout this book and in the popular press, when you hear about market risk, you are hearing about systematic risk.

The takeaway from this section is that you must have a diversified portfolio (i.e., at least thirty stocks) if you are going to invest in individual stocks. This allows you to eliminate unsystematic risk. If you follow my recommendation of investing in mutual funds with more than thirty stocks in their portfolios, you will not need to worry about unsystematic risk. The only risk you will have is systematic risk. If you are going to buy individual stocks, however, eliminating unsystematic risk is a very important consideration.

There are only a few things an economist will state with any degree of certainty, but one is that risk and return are positively correlated in the long run. In other words, as risk increases, so does long-run return. For most individuals, risk is bad—something to be avoided. How do you entice someone to take on a "bad?" You compensate them. In the stock market, this implies that the person who takes on the "bad" (i.e., the risk) should receive a higher return than the person who takes on no risk.

If I offer you a choice between A.) a 5% guaranteed return each year for ten years or B.) the same end results but in some years you may *lose* 30%, most people will choose the steady 5% gain each year. This behavior is described as individuals being "risk-averse." In other words, everything else being equal, a less-risky asset is preferred over a riskier one. In order to induce investors to put their hard-earned money into a stock that is more volatile, you have to "pay" them by having the more volatile stock yield a higher return in the end. History bears out this relationship (see the chart on page 105, summary statistics for return and risk, 1926–2009).

The quantitative people of the financial world have constructed a statistics model in which they have designated "beta" as the measurement of systematic risk. In this world, a beta of 1 represents average stock market risk. A beta of less than 1 means you have less-than-average stock market risk. For example, if your portfolio has a beta of 0.5, you have half as much systematic risk as the market. In "up" markets, your expected *return* should be half as much as the market, but in "down" markets you should *lose* half as much as the market. Similarly, if the beta of your portfolio is 2, your expected return in up markets should be two times the market return, while in down markets you will lose two times as much as the market. Beta will allow you to judge how much risk you have in your portfolio.

Risk tolerance naturally varies from individual to individual. A person who is near retirement or has little net worth and a job that is not very stable will have a much different risk tolerance (and will require a portfolio with a lower beta) than a young person who is tenured at Harvard and has a spouse who is employed at Goldman Sachs. In general, younger individuals should have a higher risk tolerance (higher beta) than older individuals (lower beta); they have more time to ride out any downturn in the stock market.

Although the above is true in general, these are not hard-and-fast rules. Individuals could be the same age, have the same job, and have the same net worth, but still not have the same tolerance for risk. Risk tolerance is an individual characteristic that can have wide variations. I teach students who are younger than twenty-five, and I am always surprised how risk-averse some say they are. These students are young and about to embark on careers that, in many cases, will be well compensated. One might expect them to have a high tolerance for risk. One reason this generation of students might be less risk tolerant than one would expect is that they may have watched their parents struggle through the financial crisis of 2008 and vowed to never be in that position.

The allocation (risk decision) of where to invest money is the toughest decision you will have to make when you construct your portfolio; it also will be the decision that will have the most influence on your expected returns. When you make the allocation decision, you will have to decide two things: what percentage of your portfolio to allocate to bonds and stocks and how to allocate the money you have set aside for stocks across their various categories. In the next chapter, I will show you an easy way to make this allocation decision. I will also explore in some detail the various options you can pursue when designing your portfolio.

SUMMARY

When it comes to investing in the stock market, there are only two things under your control: cost and allocation. Cost is the easier of the two to think about. Keep cost as low as possible. As a rule of thumb, keep the cost of your portfolio at less the 0.2%. Vanguard, one of the largest mutual fund complexes, is considered a low-cost leader. If you are thinking of buying a mutual fund, a good place to start is to find a comparable fund at Vanguard and see how the fund you might be considering matches up to what Vanguard has to offer in terms of cost and services.

The allocation decision is much harder but extremely important, as it will determine not only your risk level but also your return over time. No one can tell you what your risk tolerance should be. As I tell my students, no one knows *you* better than *you*. What is correct for person A may be completely wrong for person B.

In the next chapter, I will give you the information you need to make informed choices. The bottom line is that you need to be comfortable with the choices you make.

CHAPTER 6

INVEST TO WIN

I t is now time to reap the rewards of plowing through the first five chapters. We have completed the necessary warm-up exercises: We understand we cannot beat the market (nor can professional stock analysts), and we understand the two fundamental control variables (cost and allocation) and their importance in creating a successful portfolio. Now let's move over to the fast lane and do some real investing.

I REALLY CAN'T BELIEVE IT'S THIS SIMPLE!

In the very beginning of this book, I promised I would show you a way you could make one decision, spend no more than two hours a year, and beat the vast majority of professional stock analysts. Are you ready for the lazy investor advice? Here it is: All you have to do is pick a target retirement fund, or a target fund. Although designed for individuals to set aside money for retirement, these funds can be used for any purpose. For example, you might use a target fund to put aside money for a child's or grandchild's education. A good target fund provides broad diversification while incrementally decreasing exposure to equities and increasing exposure to bonds as the fund reaches the target date, thus reducing your risk profile.

For example, the Vanguard Target Retirement 2050 Fund holds approximately 90% of its assets in equities and 10% in bonds. This can be further broken down to 54% in a US stock index fund, 36% in an international stock index fund, 7% in a

US bond index fund, and 3% in an international bond index fund. You essentially have a piece of the whole *world* of finance in an all-in-one fund, and it satisfies all the criteria we need in a mutual fund: At 0.16%, the cost is low, and the fund has made an allocation decision based on when you think you will need the funds.

When deciding on a target date, start by considering a target fund that matches the date you anticipate withdrawing money from the fund. If you want to be more aggressive in terms of the risk you assume, you should choose a fund with a later target date; if you want to be more conservative, pick a fund with an earlier target date. For example, I am currently buying a 2060 target fund; I would be well past 100 years old in 2060, but I want the more aggressive glide path (higher risk, higher reward) that the 2060 fund gives me.

As these funds approach their target date, they have an automatic glide path away from equities (risky) to bonds (safer) assets. For example, Vanguard's target retirement funds go from a 90/10 to a 30/70 mix of stocks/bonds as they reach and go beyond the target date. This change in allocation is accomplished without the investor doing anything. This is truly the lazy way to invest, but it can also be a very smart way to participate in the stock market.

As your target date fund starts down the glide path toward a higher percentage of bonds and lower percentage of stocks, you will always have the option of moving your money to a target date fund with a later date, allowing you to continue to hold a higher percentage of stocks and lower percentage of bonds. As with any mutual funds you can withdraw any or all money at any time. Of course, with any sale of stocks you may owe taxes on your gains.

Vanguard target-date funds hit the sweet spot: They are low-cost funds, with expenses ranging from 0.14%–0.16%, and they make the important allocation decisions they consider correct for the average investor. Additional fees may apply for small accounts, and you should check with Vanguard before investing regarding any additional fees.

You can start a target-date fund at Vanguard for as little as $1,000 and add as little as $1 at any time. It is important that you set up an automatic investment plan that will permit you to take advantage of dollar-cost averaging. This automatic investment plan will force you to buy when the market is down—a time when you might not be inclined to buy stocks. If you buy a target-date fund, you will have a diversified portfolio, since you essentially own a very *small* fraction of all of the stocks in the world. If someone asks, "Do you own a piece of XYZ publicly traded company?", you can truly answer yes.

A target-date fund addresses everything we have discussed in this book and should yield very satisfactory results over the long run. Many investment complexes offer target-date funds. While I have no business relationship with Vanguard, I do own several of their funds. I have used them as examples so that you have a baseline by which to evaluate any target-date fund. Make sure you check the cost of any fund you consider and the glide path the fund uses as you approach the target date. Buy the fund you think is the most appropriate for your circumstances.

Although I am calling this the ultimate lazy way to invest, I am not doing so because I think it is a *bad* way to invest. In fact, I actually think this is a very good way for most individuals to invest in the market. Over a long period of time, the more aggressive you are with the target date, the higher the return you should expect (i.e., more risk, more reward). It could be possible that you are saving for several different reasons that will each require money at different times. For example, you could be saving for a second home, retirement, and a grandchild's education, each with different planned withdrawal dates.

In that case, you might want to invest in three different target funds.

It is important to emphasize again that you should set up an automatic investment plan so that you can take advantage of dollar-cost averaging. When you set up an automatic investment plan, the default is that you will invest at a set interval—regardless of what is happening in the market. Remember, the average investor loses 1.5%–2.0% by not buying low.

So there you have it: the ultimate lazy way to invest. Pick a good target-date mutual fund, then sit back and relax. If done correctly, you will have low costs, a "correct" allocation, and dollar-cost averaging that works for you. Also, because of the low cost structure, you will have a rate of return that will be the envy of most professional money managers.

ONLY SLIGHTLY MORE COMPLICATED ...

If you have a controlling personality and want more say about how your funds are invested, this section may be for you. If you go the route suggested in this section, you will need to do a little more work up-front, and you will need to do some rebalancing once or twice a year, but you will have the satisfaction of knowing you are in control of your allocations. This will also give you bragging rights, because there is a high probability that your rate of return will be higher than most professional investment advisors. This excess return will be partly due to the fact that you have kept costs low.

The first decision you will have to make is the allocation between a risky asset (e.g., stock mutual funds) and a less-risky asset (e.g., bond mutual funds)—in other words, your risk tolerance. This decision will have the greatest impact on your total return, so you need to make it with some careful thought. The more stock mutual funds you buy, the higher the risk and the higher the return you should receive over the long run.

Unfortunately, however, this is not a decision you can make and then forget. You will have to periodically check your allocation between these two asset classes, as the percentage allocation may change over time as the price of your stock changes. This rebalancing should be undertaken at least once a year but probably does not need to be done more than twice a year. The reason this rebalancing is required is that if you decide that a 70-30 division between stocks and bonds is optimal for you, then if stocks outperform bonds by a significant amount, your allocation could change to, say, 83-17. If this were to occur, you would need to take action to bring your allocation back in line with your desired 70-30 split. One option would be to sell some of your stock mutual funds and buy more of your bond mutual funds (i.e., sell high and buy low). If you follow this route, however, there is a complicating factor: taxes. If you are doing this rebalancing in a taxable account, you will more than likely have to pay taxes on your stock gains. You will have to weigh the benefits of getting back your "correct" allocation versus the potential tax consequences of selling an asset that has a taxable gain. If you are doing this in a tax-free retirement account, taxes will not be an issue.

Another way to move back toward the "correct" allocation is to add all new money you are investing to the fund that has an under-allocation. If you rebalance in this manner, you do not have to worry about tax consequences because you have not sold any mutual funds. This is not rocket science, where any deviation from the "correct" allocation could have devastating consequences. I would recommend rebalancing no more than twice a year and even then, *only* if there is a deviation of more than 2% or 3% from your perceived "correct" allocation. Remember, every time you rebalance, there are costs involved: your time, trading costs, and tax consequences. Rebalancing is not a free lunch.

What is the appropriate allocation between stocks and bonds? The answer is that it depends on your risk tolerance. For most of my investment career, I have allocated 100% to stocks. Warren Buffett has stated that he wants his portfolio to be allocated 90%-10% (stocks/bonds) after his death. The Vanguard target-date funds that have dates significantly in the future also have a 90%-10% mix. A more conservative approach advanced by some advisors states that the percentage of bonds you should hold ought to be the same as your age. This means that if you are forty-five years old, you should have a 55%-45% breakdown of stocks to bonds. Vanguard's target funds ultimately end up at a 30%-70% mix.

I personally think the last two breakdowns of stocks and bonds are too conservative for most individuals. Having said that, let me remind you that no one should ever talk you into taking on more risk than you can tolerate. Remember the sleep-down point? To satisfy yourself that the risk you are taking is the correct level for you, go back and review both the return and the risk that have happened over time to stocks and bonds. Although there are no guarantees for future performance, history will give you some idea of the returns—and the potential losses—you might expect over a long period. Unless you are nearing a period when you could potentially need to withdraw all your assets from your portfolio, I believe most individuals should have between 60%–100% of their portfolio in stocks. The more aggressive you want to be, the closer you will be to having 100% of your portfolio in stocks; the more conservative you want to be, the closer you will be to 60% in stocks. Remember Harry Truman's statement: "If you can't stand the heat, get out of the kitchen." If you cannot tolerate the volatility of your portfolio, reduce the percentage allocated to stocks.

Once you decide on the "correct" allocation between stocks and bonds, you must then decide where you are going to place the money you have designated for stocks and bonds. I am going to use two Vanguard funds for illustrative purposes because I think they are very good funds. They can also be used as a measuring stick to evaluate any other funds you might consider. The two funds I have chosen to illustrate how you might proceed down this path are Vanguard Total World Stock Index Fund and Vanguard Total Bond Market Index Fund.

Total World Stock holds approximately 7,000 stocks from around the world, with 51% of the portfolio from the US, 9% from emerging markets, 22% from Europe, 14% from the Pacific Rim, and the balance from the rest of the world. The expense ratio is low (0.25%), and you have diversity not only in the number of stocks but also in the countries where the money is invested.

It is important to note that for several reasons, not having international stocks in your portfolio is a mistake. Between 2001 and 2014, the percentage of global gross domestic product (GDP) accounted for by the US economy declined from 33% to 22%. Nearly 80% of all publicly traded companies domicile outside the US.[54] US equities accounted for approximately 45% of the value in the global equity market.[55] If you do not own any non-US stocks you are missing 55% of the global equity market.

Investing in non-US stocks also allows investors to gain exposure to the economies in the rest of the world. These economies will experience different economic developments than the US economy. Because the correlation coefficient is less than +1.0, this diversification leads to less volatility in your equity portfolio. Investing in international equities is a compelling strategy for diversifying your portfolio; in fact, I would argue that having at least 20% invested in non-US stocks is a necessary condition for a good equity portfolio.

For those of you who would like to have a larger percentage of your portfolio in US stocks than the 51% in Vanguard's Total World Index Fund, you can combine two Vanguard funds—Vanguard Total Stock Market Index Fund (only US stocks) and Vanguard Total International Stock Index Fund. In my opinion, if you go this route, you should have at least 20% in the Total International Index Fund. The Total Stock Market Fund is designed to provide investors with exposure to the entire US equity market, including small-, mid-, and large-cap stocks. The Total International Stock Fund offers investors a way to gain equity exposure to both developed and emerging international markets.

Whether you go the one-stop route for your stock portfolio by buying a Total World fund or the do-it-yourself route by combining a fund that only has US stocks with a Total International fund, you will have broad exposure to virtually all the equities of the world. You will have kept costs low and made an allocation decision that fits your personality.

The next step is to combine one of the above strategies with a bond fund. Once again, I will use a Vanguard fund—Vanguard Total Bond Market Index Fund—as an example by which you can judge other bond funds. The Vanguard Total Bond Fund is designed to provide broad exposure to US investment-grade bonds.[56] This fund invests approximately 30% in US corporate bonds and 70% in US government bonds in all maturity classes (short-, intermediate-, and long-term issues). This, of course, is our buffer holding. When the stock market has a substantial decline, this bond fund should have less of a decline; when the market is up substantially, this fund will be a drag on your return. The bond fund is the part that grows in percentage terms over time in a target-date retirement fund.

One might argue that there is a missing element in the above advice: an international bond exposure. In my opinion, adding an international bond fund to the above portfolio is not worth the effort of finding such a fund and keeping it at the correct allocation. Although I do not personally think it is necessary for a portfolio, if you want to add such a fund, more power to you.

I have not recommended as part of your core portfolio one of the available S&P 500 Index funds. Many investment advisors recommend such a fund as the core US fund; an S&P 500 Index fund was the first index fund I bought. Warren Buffett has stated that after his death, he wants the money that goes into equities to go into a 500 Index fund. In my opinion, the problem with this approach is that you are missing a very significant part of the market (i.e., mid- and small-cap companies). The S&P 500 Index Fund invests in 500 of the largest companies in the US. Currently, the ten largest companies in the S&P 500 are Apple, Exxon Mobil, Microsoft, Google, Johnson & Johnson, Berkshire Hathaway, Wells Fargo, General Electric, JP Morgan Chase, and Procter & Gamble. Each of these companies has had a very successful history; you do not become one of the largest companies in the US by making bad decisions.

Because they are so large, however, it is hard for them to grow much faster than the US economy as a whole. If you bought a 500 Index fund today, these ten companies, which represent 2% (10/500) of the 500 companies, would represent 17.4% of the money in the index fund. This means the other 82.6% of your money would be invested in the other 490 companies in the S&P 500—and none in the thousands of small companies that are not in the S&P 500. Some of these other companies that are not in the top 500 will be the phenomenal growth companies of the future, and you will have just missed them.

On the other hand, if you buy a Total US Stock Market Index fund, you will be buying a fund that has over 3,500 stocks, and you will have approximately 3,000 more stocks in your portfolio than if you had bought an S&P 500 Index fund. In 2014, the median market cap for the 500 largest companies was $79.3 billion; for the Total Stock Market, the market cap was $48.9 billion. As measured by market capitalization, the Total Stock Market Fund companies are approximately 40% smaller than the 500 largest companies. It is important for your portfolio to have both mid- and small-cap companies. The phenomenal-growth companies of the future are lurking somewhere in these stocks.

In summary, if you follow the advice in this section, you will be required to do more work than if you decide to buy a target-date fund. You will have to make a decision as to how much money to allocate to stocks and how much to bonds. This allocation decision is the most important decision you will make, because it will be the *main determinant* of both your return on investment and the risk in your portfolio. It would be a mistake not to have at least part of your stock portfolio invested in international stocks.

In general, your stock allocation should be between 60% and 100% of your portfolio, with the more aggressive posture being 100%. In the end, the more aggressive your portfolio, the higher the return you should receive—but your portfolio will be more volatile. The only other decision you will have to make is whether to take the default mix between foreign and domestic stocks (i.e., buy a Total World fund) or create your own mix by buying a Total US Index fund and mixing it with a Total International fund. The part of your portfolio not invested in stocks will be invested in a Total Bond Mutual fund.

This approach requires some up-front decisions on allocation and a couple of hours per year to rebalance and make sure your ideal allocation has not fallen too far out of line with what you want. It should be easy to keep the cost of this approach to less than 0.2% per year, and this approach takes care of the important things: costs and allocation.

THE FULL MONTY

This section is for those who want full control, enjoy watching what is happening in the markets, and get some pleasure out of adjusting their portfolio. These suggestions will require some time and effort on your part, especially in the beginning, but once you make a few basic decisions, it should not take more than a few hours each year to manage your portfolio. The basic reason to do the Full Monty is to tilt your portfolio to a particular asset class that *might* outperform the market even factoring in the additional risk.

I have spent a considerable amount of time trying to convince you that the stock market is semi-strong efficient. I am now going to do some backtracking. I really do believe the vast majority of stocks are fairly priced at any point in time. I also believe, however, that there are a few pockets of inefficiency in the stock market. What I am going to suggest in this section is that you *slightly* tilt your portfolio to take advantage of some of these inefficiencies, which will allow you to capture some of the above-market gains that might be available.

I am going to arbitrarily divide the world of investing into eight asset classes from which you can choose—a smorgasbord for investing. Except for the core classes, which will be identified, the asset classes you decide to invest in should not have more than 30% or less than 5% in any one-asset class: what I refer to as the 30-5 Rule.

There is absolutely no reason you should invest in all of the following asset classes. For cost reasons, when you buy any of the asset classes, you should buy them in an index fund.

Let's see the Full Monty:

- **Total US Stock Market:** This fund has been part of previous strategies. This could be one of your core funds, allowing you to disregard the 30-5 Rule. This fund should contain approximately 3,500 stocks that will give you exposure to the entire US stock market. This fund will essentially allow you to own every publicly traded company in the US. The expense ratio on such a fund can be as low as 0.05%. Even though this kind of fund will have 3,500 stocks, the largest 500 will make up approximately 3/4 of the value of the fund, thus this would be considered a large-cap blend (a balance between growth and value) fund.

- **Total World Stock:** This fund has also been part of previous strategies. This could be one of your core funds, allowing you to disregard the 30-5 Rule. This fund should contain as many as 7,000 stocks and contain stocks not only from the US but also from emerging markets, Europe, the Pacific Rim, and North America. This fund will allow you to own stock in most of the publicly traded companies in the world. The expense ratio for this kind of fund runs higher than a US-only fund. A good cost for such a fund is in the 0.30% range. Once again, this should be considered a large-cap blend fund. The advantage of this fund is you do not have to think about adding an international component.

- **Extended Market:** This is a new fund for this book. This should not be a core fund and is therefore subject to the 30-5 Rule. This kind of fund will invest in the entire US market, except for the 500 largest-cap companies. This means that this fund should have approximately 3,000 stocks and will allow you to essentially own all of the publicly traded mid- and small-cap stocks in the US. The expense ratio of such a fund should be in the range of 0.10%. This should be considered a mid-cap blend fund. The reason you should consider this fund for a portion of your portfolio is that over long periods, mid- and small-cap stocks tend to outperform their big brothers. I consider this one of the "tilt" asset classes. This asset class will potentially allow you to outperform the market. You might call this a "bragging rights" class of stocks, because it can potentially allow you to outperform the market.

- **Small-Cap Value**: This is a new fund for this book. This should not be one of your core funds and is therefore subject to the 30-5 Rule. This fund will invest in small-cap companies that are temporarily out of favor with Wall Street. This fund should have half of the small-cap market, or about 800 stocks. This, of course, should be considered a small-cap value fund and is the ultimate tilt fund. The expense ratio of such a fund should be in the 0.10% range. Academic research has shown that over long periods, small-cap value funds outperform the market risk—even after adjusting for the higher risk level. These small-cap funds can be a volatile segment of the market, thus investment in this segment of the market can give you a bumpy ride on "the Street." For those of you who can tolerate the swings in the market, this is an interesting choice for your portfolio. In the long run, the bumpy ride should allow you to enjoy above-average returns.

- **Total International Stock:** We have reviewed this fund before in this book. This should not be a core fund, thus subject to the 30-5 Rule. If you are using Total World as your core fund, this fund may not be necessary. If, instead, you are using Total Stock as your core, this fund is essential. This fund invests in the world equity markets and can have 6,000 stocks. A reasonable fee on such an account should be as low as 0.15%. Most investment advisors consider owning some foreign stocks as essential for a well-balanced portfolio. The diversification that foreign stock gives a portfolio can help dampen the swing of the portfolio.
- **REIT:** REIT stands for real estate investment trusts. We have not seen this fund before in this book. This should not be a core fund, and is therefore subject to the 30-5 rule. A good starting point for expenses would be in the 0.12% range. REITs are companies that purchase office buildings, hotels, health care facilities, and other real estate property. REITs have often performed differently from stocks and bonds, so this kind of fund may offer some diversification to a portfolio already made up of stocks and bonds. The diversification factor would be the main attraction of investing in a REIT.
- **Total Bond:** We have reviewed this fund before. This is one of two funds in which I suggest you invest the bond portion of your allocation decision. It is important that you keep the risk in this fund to a minimum. Its main purpose is to serve as

a buffer to the more volatile stock market. The fund should have the vast majority of its assets invested in US government bonds of all maturities and no more than 30% invested in investment-grade corporate bonds. Expense ratios should be in the 0.07% range. An option here could be to buy a mutual fund that invests in below-investment-grade bonds, sometimes called high-yield corporate bonds. Although this type of mutual fund can have twice the yield of a Total Bond fund, in my opinion, it is not worth the additional risk. If you want to take on more risk, do it in equities.

- **Inflation-Protected Bond:** This is a new fund to this book. I consider this a complement to a Total Bond fund. I would suggest that most, if not all, of your bond money be placed in a Total Bond fund. By investing in bonds that provide a "real" rate of return, an inflation-protected bond fund is designed to protect investors from the eroding effect of inflation. These bonds are backed by the full faith and credit of the federal government, and the principal of the bonds is adjusted quarterly, based on inflation. As of 2016, we are currently in a low-inflation period, so these bonds do not provide many advantages to investors, but if inflation raises its ugly head, these bonds would protect you from losing your purchasing power. Cost should run in the range of 0.20%.

Name of Fund	Type of Fund	Invest-ments	Core or 30-5?	A Tilt Fund?	Essential?
Total US Stock Market	Large-cap US blend	All US stocks	Core, with Total Interna-tional	No	Yes—unless using Total World, then must use with Interna-tional
Total World Stock	Large-cap world blend	All world stocks	Core (does not require Total Stock or Interna-tional)	No	Yes—can replace Total Stock and Inter-national
Extended Market	Mid-cap US blend	All US stocks except the largest 500	30-5 Rule applies	Yes	No—only use to tilt portfolio
Small-Cap Value	Small-cap US value	Smallest-cap US stocks	30-5 Rule applies	Yes (this is the ulti-mate tilt fund)	No—only use to tilt portfolio
Total Interna-tional	All non-US stocks	All stocks of the world except US	Core (must be used with Total US)	No	Must be used if using Total Stock Fund
REIT	Real estate US stock	Index of US real estate	30-5 Rule applies	No	No
Total Bond	Index US bonds	Holds an index of US bonds	Core (basic decision on mix between stocks and bonds)	No	Yes—if using less than 100% stocks
Inflation-Protected Bond	Inflation-protection US bonds	Index of US infla-tion-pro-tection US bonds	30-5 Rule applies	No	No

So there you have the Full Monty: eight very specific investment options. The only thing you need to do is decide which ones to use and how much money to put in each. The first six funds are stock mutual funds, and you should have between 60% and 100% of your portfolio in these six funds. The core stock investment should be in a Total US Stock or a Total World fund. If you use a Total US Stock fund, then you will also need to use a Total International fund. The extended market and small-cap value funds will tilt your portfolio so you can exploit market inefficiencies and add diversification; the REIT fund will add diversification to your portfolio. The balance of your portfolio should be in the two bond funds, with the majority (if not all) of this bond money in a Total Bond fund.

One of the many good things about the Full Monty is that it allows you to have diversification across asset classes, and diversification can help reduce the volatility of a portfolio. The element critical to reducing volatility by adding an asset class to a portfolio is the *correlation coefficient*. The correlation coefficient is always between +1.0 and -1.0.

+1.0 means the two elements are perfectly correlated (i.e., they move in lockstep in the same direction), while -1.0 means they move in lockstep but in opposite directions.

If I buy 100 shares of GE on 1/8/2016 and another 100 shares on 1/8/2017, these two purchases have done nothing to reduce the volatility of my portfolio. The correlation coefficient is +1.0, so the risk has not been reduced with the second purchase.

On the other hand, if I have a choice between two risky assets with the following characteristics, I can reduce my risk to zero. Assume there is a sunscreen company that earns 30% when there is a sunny season and loses 10% during a rainy season. Also, assume there is a rain hat company that earns 30% during a rainy season and loses 10% during a sunny season.

Assume that the probability of the season being rainy or sunny is 50/50.

If I buy only one of the assets, then I will have a 50% chance of making 30% and a 50% chance of losing 10% in any one year. If I buy only one of these assets, then the *arithmetic mean return* over long periods of time is 10% ((30% – 10%)/2). In half of the years, I will make 30%, and in the other half of the years, I will lose 10%. If I buy one of these assets, my portfolio will be volatile.

On the other hand, if I invest $1 in both firms, I will make 10% every year, regardless of the weather. Each year, I will make 30% on one investment and lose 10% on the other. Thus, I make 20% (30% – 10%) on my $2 investment, or a fixed 10% (20%/2) per year. By combining these two very risky assets, I have reduced my risk to zero (i.e., I always earn 10%).

This amazing result is accomplished because the correlation coefficient between these two assets is –1.0. This result can be verified with the following formula:

$$\sigma_p^2 = \sum_{j=1}^{n} \sum_{i=1}^{n} w_j\, w_i\, \text{Cov}\, (r_i,\, r_j)$$

Aren't you glad you don't have to do the mathematics?

Unfortunately, it is not possible to find asset classes that have a -1.0 correlation coefficient. This is still good news, however, in that anytime you have assets with a correlation coefficient of less than 1.0, you can reduce the risk of the portfolio by *combining those assets*. The asset classes listed above do not have a correlation coefficient of 1.0; hence, when you combine these asset classes, you reduce the volatility of your stock portfolio. This is one of the primary advantages of the Full Monty.

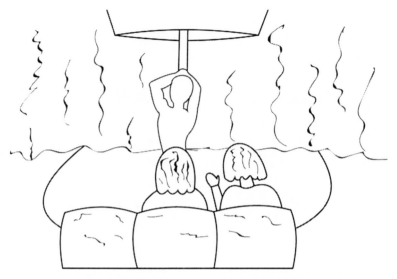

My stock full Monty is not as exciting as this full Monty!

I WANT TO SEE THE FULL MONTY!

All the major mutual fund complexes offer all the asset classes described in the Full Monty. Vanguard is the largest of these fund complexes and is where I have most of my investments. Vanguard is considered by many in the investment world to be *the* index and low-cost leader. It is very convenient to have all your investments under one roof, so if you find a complex you like that has all the asset classes you want at a reasonable cost, go for it.

The other fund complex I will mention is Dimensional Fund Advisors, an investment complex that uses academic research to construct their mutual fund portfolios. Eugene Fama and Kenneth French, two of the most well-known academics in the investment field, serve as advisors to Dimensional. Fama has won a Nobel Prize in economics for his work in investments, and French is widely quoted throughout the investment world. Dimensional overweighs small-cap and value stocks in many of its portfolios, resulting in a tilt to where they perceive you can earn above-market returns. Sound familiar? The one problem I have with Dimensional is not the fees they charge but the fact that investors can only purchase the funds by going through an investment advisor. The advisor you use will tack on another fee for the services he or she provides. If you are smart and wisely use the information you have read in this book, you will not need a financial advisor to help you allocate money among the various investment assets and tilt your portfolio toward market inefficiencies. If you tilt your portfolio to small-value stocks, you should beat almost all professional money managers—without using a financial advisor.

THE FULL MONTY COMPLETELY EXPOSED

In this section, I am going to give two very specific examples of how you could implement an investment strategy doing the Full Monty. One will be aggressive, and the other will be more conservative. First, the more aggressive strategy, where the investor has decided a 90-10 stock-bond split is optimum. The following list is written as the percentage allocation to a fund, the name of the fund, the mutual fund ticker symbol, and the expense ratio.

STOCKS 90%
50% / Vanguard Total World Stock Index / VTXSX / 0.27%
20% / Vanguard Extended Market Index Fund Admiral Shares/ VEXAX / 0.10%
15% / Vanguard Small-Cap Value Index Fund Admiral / VSIAX / 0.09%
5% / Vanguard REIT Index Fund Admiral Shares / VSIX / 0.12%

BONDS 10%
10% / Vanguard Total Bond Market Index Admiral Shares / VBTLX / 0.07%

The cost of this portfolio is approximately 0.18% per year—well within our target cost range. We have roughly 25% of the portfolio in international stocks through the Total World Fund; 25% in large-cap US stocks (also in the Total World Fund); 20% in mid-cap in the Extended Market Fund; 15% in small-cap value; 5% in real estate; and the final 10% in bonds. This is a well-diversified portfolio that has a tilt toward mid- and small-cap value stocks, which should allow an investor to exploit the market inefficiencies.

A more conservative portfolio might look like this:

STOCKS 60%
30% / Vanguard Total Stock Market Index Fund Admiral Shares / VTSAX / 0.05%
20% / Vanguard Total International Stock Index Fund Admiral Shares / VTIAX / 0.14%
10% / Vanguard Small-Cap Index Fund Admiral Shares / VSIAX / 0.09%

BONDS 40%
30% / Vanguard Total Bond Market Index Funds Admiral Shares / VBTLX / 0.07%
10% / Vanguard Short-Term Inflation-Protected Securities Index / VTAPX / 0.10%

The cost of this portfolio is 0.08%, which is amazing, given that you own a fraction of almost all the stocks of the world, have a portion of your portfolio devoted to small-cap value stocks, and own a percentage of almost all US investment-grade bonds. This portfolio also has a tilt toward the inefficiencies in the market, which should allow you to outperform the market. This tilt, plus the very low expense ratio, should allow you to do very well over the long run.

AN AFTERTHOUGHT

I gave a copy of the first draft of this book to my good friend Jinsie and asked her to read it. Her reaction was that nowhere in the book did I mention dividends or interest payments; she was curious why I had chosen not to cover these two important concepts. The problem with dividends and interest is they create taxable events when payments are made to the investor. Everything else being equal, during the accumulation phase of investing, you should want companies to *retain their earnings* and to wisely invest these retained earnings in new opportunities for the company. This should allow the company to grow earnings. When you do sell, the stock price should have grown over time, and your long-term capital gains will be taxed at preferential rates—instead of at regular rates like dividends and interest payments.

I would guess the real question Jinsie wanted to ask was, what should you do if you are not in the accumulation phase of life and must rely on your portfolio for current income? Even in this case, I would not change my recommendation, as stocks have historically outperformed bonds over the entire business cycle—not every year, but over the *entire cycle*.

I do not think anyone can afford not to have a significant portion of their portfolio in stocks. The 2060 Vanguard Target Retirement Fund has a current yield of approximately 2%. If you buy a fund like this, some of the stocks in the portfolio will pay a high dividend, and some will pay no dividend; hence, you will receive dividends from the mutual fund and still have the potential for long-term growth. Remember, Warren Buffett wants his estate invested 90% in stocks and only 10% in bonds.

I have often joked that my financial planning goal was to have the check to the undertaker bounce. If you know precisely when you are going to die and do not plan to leave any money to anyone or anything, then you can ignore the above advice. If this is not the case, you need to have stocks in your portfolio.

SUMMARY

This chapter has presented three basic options for investing in the market. These options range from the very simple (where you can spend less than one hour each year making sure you have the correct target-date mutual fund) to the Full Monty (where you might spend two or three hours per year rebalancing your portfolio). All three options allow you to control allocation and risk while keeping cost significantly below the average fees charged by investment advisors. Remember, cost and allocation are the two variables you *can* control. The dollars you save by not paying a high fee to an investment advisor are dollars you can keep in your account. You can think of this money going toward your own boat payment—rather than to your advisor's.

JUST DO IT!

In summary, everything I have learned about investing over the past forty years can be summed up in two strategies: Keep cost low, and allocate your investments wisely. What is amazing is that you can satisfy both conditions with a good target-date mutual fund. As I tell my economics students, it is the job of economists to make common sense complicated. That is why the final exam for the investments course is so difficult.

Although there are only two guiding principles you need to remember as you travel down Wall Street, do not forget the preparations you need to make before you start your trip.

1. Pay off all credit card debt.
2. Review your insurance requirements.
3. Explore ways in which you can use retirement plans to minimize taxes, and take full advantage of any match to those plans offered by your employer.
4. Consider the rent-vs.-buy housing decision.

Also, do not forget the other lessons you have learned in this book.

- Avoid collectibles as an investment vehicle.
- The stock market is basically semi-strong efficient.
- Buy low-cost index funds.
- Do not try to time the market; the market is a random walk.
- Make dollar-cost averaging work for you by using an automatic reinvestment plan.

- For fun and profit, tilt your portfolio to capture some market inefficiencies (i.e., small-cap value stocks).
- Invest in the stock market for projects that are at least five years in the future.
- Start early to invest, and let the power of compounding work for you.
- The decision that will have the most impact on your long-run rate of return is the allocation decision you make (i.e., stocks vs. bonds).
- Don't be a market plunger: Invest any "manna from heaven" in the market over an extended period of time (i.e., use dollar-cost averaging for lottery winnings).

So there you have it: everything you wanted to know about investing but didn't know who to ask. If you follow the guidelines in this book, you will have a market return that is superior to almost everyone who invests in the stock market.

If you follow the rules outlined in this book, it would not be unreasonable to assume that you can earn a 10% before-tax return over an extended period. If you are the typical consumer who buys high, sells low, and pays your investment advisor 1%, you might expect a 7% return with the same market conditions. If you can set aside $1,000 a month for thirty years, the difference would be *more than $1 million*. Not a bad investment for the price of this book!

Gross return	Investment per month	Number of years	Balance after 30 years
10% (savvy investor)	$1,000	30	$2,279,325
7% (typical investor)	$1,000	30	$1,227,087

Remember, above all else: **BUY LOW, SELL HIGH!**

GLOSSARY

401(k) & 403(b): Defined-contribution retirement plans which allow an employee to set aside money tax-free and accumulate tax-free returns until the money is withdrawn at retirement.

529 plan: A tax-advantaged savings plan designed to encourage saving for future college costs. Money invested is after-tax money, but the return in a 529 accumulates tax-free and is never taxed if withdrawn for qualified educational expenses.

Actively managed mutual fund: A mutual fund that hires a portfolio manager who attempts to find undervalued stocks so the investor in the mutual fund will earn above-market returns.

Beta: A measure of the volatility or systematic risk of a security or a portfolio. A beta of one indicates that the security's price or portfolio moves with the same volatility as the average stock.

Broker: A broker is an agent who arranges transactions between a buyer and seller for a commission. Brokers are only required to offer a product that is suitable for their clients.

Defined benefit (DB) retirement plan: A type of retirement plan in which an employer promises a specified monthly benefit at retirement that is determined by earnings history and length of service. A DB plan is unusual in today's work environment.

Defined contribution (DC) retirement plan: A type of retirement plan in which the employer, employee, or both make contributions to an account that can be used when the employee retires. A DC is what most working individuals currently have.

Dollar-cost averaging: A technique of buying a fixed dollar amount on a regular schedule. The investor purchases more shares when prices are low and fewer shares when prices are high.

Dow Jones Industrial Average (DJIA), or Dow: A price-weighted average of thirty large companies. The DJIA was formulated by Charles Dow in 1896.

Efficient markets hypothesis (EMH): An investment theory which states that all stocks reflect all relevant information; hence, one cannot beat the market, because all stocks are fairly priced. Although there are three forms of the efficient market hypothesis, EMH most commonly refers to the semi-strong form.

Fiduciary duty: A fiduciary duty is the highest standard of care. Fiduciaries must remove all conflicts and must not profit from their position.

Free rider: A person who buys stocks knowing that those stocks are fairly priced due to the semi-strong form of the efficient market hypothesis. Hence, he or she can purchase a stock knowing that it is fairly priced without having any expense of searching for an undervalued stock.

Fundamental analysis: A method of evaluating a security in an attempt to measure its intrinsic value. A fundamental analyst will use financial and other qualitative and quantitative factors to find the intrinsic value.

Hedge funds: A limited partnership of high-net-worth individuals that invests in a variety of assets, often with complex portfolio construction.

High-deductible health plan: A health plan which has a higher deductible but lower premiums than a traditional health insurance plan. You will pay more of your health care costs before the insurance company starts to pay its share.

Marginal tax rate: The proportion of the last dollar of income taxed by the government.

Market capitalization, or market cap: The market value of a company's outstanding shares. Market cap is calculated by taking the stock price and multiplying it by the total number of shares outstanding. Market cap is often broken down into three categories: large-cap, mid-cap, and small-cap.

Mutual funds: An investment vehicle made up of a pool of money collected from a group of investors for the purpose of investing in an agreed upon manner.

NASDAQ: The second-largest stock exchange in the world. The NASDAQ is located in New York City. In general, smaller companies are first traded on the NASDAQ and are then traded on the New York Stock Exchange.

New York Stock Exchange (NYSE): The world's largest stock exchange and where most major companies stocks are traded.

Passively managed index mutual fund: A mutual fund that simply buys all stocks in an index, thus duplicating the return of the chosen index. An index mutual fund provides broad market exposure, low operating expenses, and low portfolio turnover.

Random walk hypothesis: A hypothesis which states that past price movements cannot be used to predict future price movements. If the random walk hypothesis holds, then technical analysis will not help find undervalued stocks.

Regression to the mean: A technical way of saying that things trend to even out over time. Specifically, it refers to the tendency of a random variable to return to "normal" over repeated tests.

Roth IRA: A type of retirement plan that allows an individual to set aside after-tax money into a retirement account. All money withdrawn at retirement—including gains—is not taxed.

Self-employed plans (SEP): A type of retirement plan that allows self-employed individuals to set aside pretax money into a retirement plan and accumulate gains tax-free until the money is withdrawn at retirement.

Semi-strong form of the efficient market hypothesis: A form of the efficient market hypothesis which states that all public information is reflected in a stock's current price, meaning neither fundamental nor technical analysis can be used to achieve above-average returns.

Standard & Poor's 500, or S&P 500: A stock market index based on the market capitalizations of 500 large companies. It is a common benchmark for US stock market performance.

Strong form of the efficient market hypothesis: A form of the efficient market hypothesis which states that *all* information, whether public or private, is reflected in a stock's price. The strong form means that not even insider information can give an investor an advantage.

Systematic risk, or market risk: The risk inherent in stock market investing. Systematic risk consists of the day-to-day fluctuations in a stock's price.

Technical analysis: A method of evaluating stocks that uses past market data (primarily price and volume) to predict the movement of stock prices.

Traditional IRA: A type of retirement plan that allows an individual to set aside pretax income and accumulate gains, tax-free, until the money is withdrawn.

Undervalued stocks: Stocks that are temporarily priced below their true value.

Unsystematic risk: Risk specific to a particular stock. This type of risk can be reduced through diversification.

Weak form of the efficient market hypothesis: A form of the efficient market hypothesis which claims that past price movements and volume data do not affect stock prices. This means that the stock market is a random walk, and technical analysis will not help identify undervalued stocks.

INDEX

full retirement age, 52, 54, 60

future of social security, 20, 62

standard deviation, 111

stock returns 1926-2009, 111, 114

strong form EMH, 80, 86

suitable product, 49

superman, 104

systematic risk, 112

Tarzan and Jane, 106

tax penalty retirement account, 25

taxes, 4, 20, 21, 24, 29, 47, 118, 121

technical analysis, 80, 86

thirty – five rule 30-5, 127

three-factor model, 94

Uncle Sam, 21, 24, 31

umbrella liability insurance policy, 12, 35

unsystematic risk, 112

Vanguard funds, 105, 117, 122, 135

value stocks, 94, 136

Warren Buffett, 72, 89, 98, 102, 122

weak form of the EMH, 80, 82

when to collect social security, 53

wills, 34

End Notes

1. Anyone can call himself or herself a financial advisor. For a humorous look at what it takes to be a financial advisor, see episode 74 of *Last Week Tonight with John Oliver* (HBO). You can print a bachelor of financial advising degree from Oliver's website.

2. A defined-contribution (DC) plan is a type of retirement plan in which the employer, employee, or both make contributions on a regular basis. In a defined-contribution plan, future benefits fluctuate based on the investment returns the individual earns. The employee makes the decision where the money should be invested.

3. The website of the Council For Disability Awareness, "Chance of Disability"

4. "Driven by Campaign Populism, Democrats Unite on Expanding Social Security," *New York Times*, June 18, 2016

5. "Social Security: A Program and Policy History," Social Security Office of Policy, http://www.ssa.gov/policy/docs/ssb/v66n1/v66n1p1.html

6. "Ida May Fuller, 100, of Vermont, Received First Social Security Check: Classmate of Calvin Coolidge," *Washington Post*, January 31, 1975

7. "A Summary of the 2016 Annual Reports," Social Security Administration, http://www.ssa.gov/oact/trsum/

8. Harvey S. Rosen and Ted Gayer, *Public Finance, 9th Edition* (McGraw-Hill/Irwin, 2009), p. 235

9. If your state has an income tax, this may also save you on the tax you pay your state.

10. *Dimensional Matrix Book 2015*, p. 66

11. "100 Years of Inflation-Adjusted Housing Price History," Observations, http://observationsandnotes.blogspot.com/2011/07/housing-prices-inflation-since-1900.html

12. "Apple Market Cap," YCharts, https://ycharts.com/companies/AAPL/market_cap

13. The WisdomTree website, a blog by Jeremy Schwartz, October 22, 2013

14. The definition of industrials has changed over time to now include companies like Goldman Sachs and Visa.

15. An advanced course will cover what they have to do when they add or drop companies from the index.

16. For a more comprehensive look at Social Security, see Rosen and Gayer's *Public Finance*, chapter 11.

17. "What Is The Maximum Social Security Retirement Benefit Payment," Social Security Administration, www.sss.gov/what-is-the-maximum-social-security-retirement-benefit-payment

18. "Retirement Benefits," Social Security Administration, www.ssa.gov/retire/

19. Laurence J. Kotlikoff, Philip Moeller, and Paul Solman, *Get What's Yours: The Secrets to Maxing Out Your Social Security* (Simon and Schuster, 2015)

20. "Valuing Social Security Benefits As An Asset on the Household Balance Sheet," from the blog by Michael Kitces, https://www.kitces.com/blog/valuing-social-security-benefits-as-an-asset-on-the-household-balance-sheet/

21. Kotlikoff, Moeller, and Solman, *Get What's Yours*, p. 15

22. An actuarially fair return means an insurance plan that on average pays out the same amount that is receives in contributions.

23. Ibid., pp. 16–17

24. "People Lack Confidence in Having Enough Money to Live Comfortably During Retirement," StreetInsider, http://www.streetinsider.com

25. Kotlikoff, Moeller, and Solman, *Get What's Yours*, p. 13

26. Allan Sloan, "When Should You Start Cashing In On Social Security," *Fortune Magazine*, December 4, 2013

27. Financial Engines (an investment advice company) recently updated its free online Social Security calculator that will help you explore various outcomes of filing for Social Security.

28. Kotlikoff, Moeller, and Solman, *Get What's Yours*, p. 84

29. *The Economist*, June 7, 2010

30. "Reports and Studies: 1938 Advisory Council," Social Security Administration, https://www.ssa.gov/history/reports/38advise.html

31. "A Summary of the 2016 Annual Reports," Social Security Administration, http://www.ssa.gov/oact/trsum

32. Kotlikoff, Moeller, and Solman, *Get What's Yours*, pp. 188–89

33. "Who's poor in America?", Pew Research Center, http://www.pewresearch.org/fact-tank/2014/01/13/whos-poor-in-america-50-years-into-the-war-on-poverty-a-data-portrait/

34. John Maynard Keynes, *The General Theory of Employment, Interest and Money* (London: McMillian and Co., 1936), p. 158

35. "Stock Market Crash of 2008," The Balance, http://useconomy.about.com/od/Financial-Crisis/a/Stock-Market-Crash-2008.htm

36. Ilia D. Dichev, *What Are Stocks Investors' Actual Historical Return?* (University of Michigan, 2004), p. 2

37. *A Practical Approach to Low-cost Investing*, a blog by Rick Ferri, June 13, 2013

38. Alexandria Stevenson, *New York Times*, May 5, 2014

39. Eugene F. Fama, "Efficient Capital Markets: A Review of Theory and Empirical Work," *Journal of Finance*, May 1970, pp. 383–417

40. *2014 Investment Company Fact Book*, chapter 2

41. Jeff Sommer, *New York Times*, March 14, 2015

42. Zvi Bodie, Alex Kane, and Alan J. Marcus, *Essentials of Investments: Ninth Edition* (McGraw-Hill, September 25, 2012), pp. 281–82

43. Burton Malkiel, *A Random Walk Down Wall Street* (W. W. Norton & Company, 2012), p. 157

44. F. Galton, "Vox populi," *Nature*, Issue 75, pp. 450–51

45. Transcript of Rex Sinquefield's opening statement in debate with Donald Yacktman at the Schwab Institutional Conference in San Francisco, October 12, 1995

46. research-spiva-institutional-scorecard-how-much-do-fees-affect-the-active-versus-passive-debate.pdf

47. *Fortune*, April 3, 1995

48. The MarketWatch.com website, March 13, 2014

49. Eugene Fama and Kenneth French, "Multifactor Explanations of Asset Pricing Anomalies," *Journal of Finance*, Issue 51, pp. 55–84

50. William Sharpe, "Likely Gains from Market Timing," *Financial Analysts Journal*, Vol. 31, no. 2 (1975)

51. H. Nejat Seyhun, "Stock Market Extremes and Portfolio Performance," for Towneley Capital Management, 1994

52. Warren Buffet, "Berkshire Hathaway Inc.: 1997 Chairman's Letter," http://www.berkshirehathaway.com/letters/1997.html

53. John Bogle, *Bogle on Mutual Funds: New Perspectives for the Intelligent Investor* (Dell, 1994), p. 235

54. http://www.investopedia.com/articles/markets/011916/investing-us-stocks-vs-international-stocks-2016.asp

55. https://personal.vanguard.com/pdf/icriecr.pdf, p.2

56. Generally, investment-grade bonds are judged by the rating agencies as likely to meet payment obligations, such that banks are allowed to invest in them.

CPSIA information can be obtained
at www.ICGtesting.com
Printed in the USA
FFOW02n1847260217
32870FF

9 781457 548222